THE

SECRET

APARTMENT

Vet Stadium, a surreal memoir

TOM GARVEY

ISBN: 9798567207994

Editorial advice and proofreading suggestions by Hugh Gilmore, Lorraine McGrath, Amanda Blazic, Sheila Weinstein, Sueann Rybak, and my wife Peggy were both much needed and gratefully accepted.
Cover art provided by Brian Groth, Artwithanedge1@yahoo.com
 Photo of Tom and Mozie (back cover) courtesy of Len Lear and *The Chestnut Hill Local.*

www.happyselfpublisher.com

The Secret Apartment is dedicated to everyone who worked at Veterans Stadium in any capacity or at any level in putting on "The Show," and for the fans who suffered bad weather, press and heartbreaking seasons with courage and grace.

TABLE OF CONTENTS

PREFACE

The Secret Apartment is an unintended memoir. It began as a way to amuse friends in a time of stress, isolation, and fear; a diversion, written for close friends in the spring of 2020 as America began to quarantine for the Pandemic and the deadly COVID-19 Virus. We had no idea how bad things were going to be or how long isolation and social distancing might last. It was frightening and my only intention was to provide friends with a momentary diversion and some amusement in hard times. This "diversion" came to life as something I had to share with others.

The first posting was on March 31st, 2020. Every three or four days I would post another short story about The Secret Apartment. In June, Lois Hoffman, The Happy Self Publisher, noted I had accumulated over 40,000 words and I began working on *The Secret Apartment* as a memoir, to be presented as a collection of short stories. Nothing has been made up and to the best of my knowledge and memory everything presented is both true and correct, though not necessarily always in chronological order.

I hope you enjoy these stories as much as I enjoyed living them.

Tom Garvey
Ambler, Pennsylvania

THE SECRET APARTMENT

If I overheard anyone telling this story in a bar or at a party, I wouldn't believe it either. But I must confess, I'd probably "scooch" a little closer, eavesdropping, unable to walk away. I'd have to find out how this yarn unraveled.

Let's begin an implausible story with a seemingly simple yet complex question.

If you were single, never married with no children or dependents, would you, if you had the opportunity, have lived "on the down low" in a secret apartment in Veterans Stadium?

In this proposal we have an off the wall South Philly version of "The Phantom of the Opera," but the larger notion this question begs could easily challenge the inner demons of sports fans anywhere. If you had an opportunity to live in a major sports stadium of a team you grew up loving, what would you have done?

In my case: I could, so I did.

"Truth, always strange, is stranger than fiction."
~ Lord Byron

I lived on the ground level of Veterans Stadium, beneath the slope of the 300-level seats, in left field from October 2nd, 1979 until the last days of 1981. My apartment was on the 200-level concourse in what had originally been intended to be a novelty stand. There were 60 concession stands in the stadium, 48 for food and beverages and 12 for novelties. I had the only key to a former novelty stand on the 200-level concourse beneath the seats in section-354 in left field above the visiting team's bullpen. This former novelty stand had so little business the year the Vet opened it had been shut down and not used since late summer 1971.

I knew I had the only key to the cavernous room because I changed the lock. I even received mail at the stadium delivered to the concession offices underground on the 100-level. Occasionally I received cards from friends addressed simply to: "Tom Garvey, Vet Stadium, 19148."

That's admittedly bizarre and I'll come back to it later because we have other hotdogs to fry here.

My living at the Vet was in no way authorized or legal, and had I been caught, a grievously serious tsunami of grief would have swept me God knows where. Life would've gotten ugly.

I dealt with any fears a reasonable person might have in an unreasonable way, I simply ignored them. I tried to never dwell on the various factions that justifiably would have come down on me, jostling in line, hungering for their pound of flesh. It would have been a long, angry queue, but screaming and furiously pushing their way to the front of the line would've been the two hysterically angry red-faced men I feared most, and with good reason: they were my mother's brothers.

Two of my uncles worked at the stadium. They sold hot dogs. This was how they earned an exceptionally good living and supported their families. They'd been selling hotdogs at sporting events for more than a generation. They were exceptionally good at it. My uncles sold tons of hotdogs and didn't deserve to be blindsided. They had vouched for me and gotten me my job at the stadium. Tug McGraw once told me, while laughing so hard he almost fell off his barstool at Jack's Firehouse, up near the old prison in Fairmount, that had I been caught, he visualized my uncles feeding me into the machine at Medford's Meats that made the millions of hotdogs consumed at the Vet. Tugger vividly described me disappearing bite-by-bite slathered in neon yellow mustard high atop the 700-level.

Tug loved telling stories, and he was enjoying himself. He choked on his words when he described my coffin as a hotdog roll. McGraw was kidding of course, but I knew he had a point.

UNCLES

Here is a little background on my uncles because these men who had mastered the art of selling hot dogs were the key to my being at the Vet in the first place.

After World War II, my Mother's four brothers were scrambling to find work. Only one of them, Joe, had a job and during a potluck dinner at one of their apartments, Joe made the offhand comment the weather was so bitterly cold on his construction site he thought some of the guys would've almost killed for a hot cup of coffee.

Next morning his three brothers who hadn't found work borrowed my Mother's `46 Plymouth Coupe, removed the backseat, and sold hot coffee through a hole they cut in the fence.

A construction worker asked, "Wouldn't have anything to eat in the trunk of your car would you, forgot my lunch?" Two of my uncles answered at once, "We will tomorrow." The brothers' profit that first day came to twenty-eight dollars and change. Within a few days, the foreman on the job recognized the collateral benefits of workers staying on site and not running off to a taproom down the road for a sandwich and a few beers, often coming back drunk or not at all. The foreman let my uncles "jerry-rig" a small olive-green Army surplus trailer against his fence. Bob, who had been in the Army, had a connection and they got three for $75.00. My uncles only needed one trailer, but the deal was for three, so they began looking for a few more construction sites and so it began. Their little "hole in the fence" operation increased job by job, and by hard work and a hell of a lot of timing and luck, growing into one of the largest sports and industrial catering firms in the nation. They wrote the book on an evolving form of catering as they lived it.

When I told you my uncles "Sold a ton of hotdogs" it wasn't hyperbole. I was "putting you on." From that first day working out of my mother's car, her brothers' business mushroomed into on-the-job feeding at several oil refineries and construction sites in the Philadelphia area. At the same time they began catering high school football games for the entire Philadelphia Catholic League, both city and suburbs, and most insanely and improbably after only a few years in the business, catering the Army-Navy Game held every year in Philly's Municipal Stadium. This meant feeding over 105,000 ravenous football fans. Bob Nilon won the contract when he got a sit-down with an Admiral in the Naval Academy. Bob served in the South Pacific as an intelligence officer during World War II. An Army buddy he'd served with was related to the Admiral and through this contact Bob passed a request for a three-minute meeting to explain how he and his brothers could not only handle the concessions but also dramatically increase sales. The Admiral, an avid hockey fan, followed and played hockey all his life. He had a hockey puck on his desk as a paperweight. The meeting started off with a casual comment by Bob about hockey. When the Admiral learned Bob had not only been an incredible hockey star in college but had won the coveted Hobey Baker Trophy in the 1938-1939 season for "Most goals and assists" while playing for Saint Nicholas Men's Amateur Hockey Club in New York, the conversation took a "drop the puck" turn and the men bonded. After he learned Bob Nilon would've been on the American Olympic Hockey Team in 1940 had it not been for World

War II, Bob probably could have walked out of the meeting with a contract no matter what he proposed. But Bob scored the opportunity of a lifetime not only because of his gift of gab and hockey exploits, but because his proposal was simplicity itself. It was sheer inspirational genius: Division of labor to increase efficiency. Up till then, to purchase a hotdog or drink, customers stood in an often rowdy crowd at the counter to place their order. A server would fill their request, collect money and make change. Bob's proposal was for the servers to never handle money but simply fill the order, moving on to the next consumer. The customer would then stand in line to pay a cashier. The Admiral loved the idea and enjoyed listening to the earnest redheaded combat vet. Bob had even been an Eagle Scout but sealed the deal when he asked for a one-year "drop dead" contract if he couldn't honor his commitment to dramatically increase sales. If I said Bob scored something akin to a hat trick that day, I'd be shaving points. Nilon Brothers catered every Army-Navy Game, but one from 1950 to 1986. It was kismet, putting Nilon Brothers Caterers on the board as major players.

First day they sold coffee through a hole in the fence out of the trunk of my mother's car they made almost thirty dollars, not bad money for the time. The evening after The Army-Navy Game only a few years later found them sitting around my mom's dining room table, giddily counting over $33,000 in small bills, teetering stacks of money everywhere. They laughed until they cried. It was nuts, but the good kind.

My uncles catered national golf tournaments, college football games and even nailed another exclusive long-term contract for The Pennsylvania Farm Show Buildings in Harrisburg, 24 acres under roof in 11 buildings with over a half-million visitors for the Farm Show alone with other events almost weekly throughout the year. The buildings were rarely dark.

The Army-Navy Game connection and Nilon's growing on-the-job feeding reputation led to another golden opportunity to provide all food services for over 37,000 construction workers building the Savannah River Project on 310 square miles near Aiken, South Carolina. Dupont and the United States Government were going to build H-Bombs. The construction phase projected to last less than three years. Once security fences, roads, utilities, buildings and all necessary improvements were completed, the U.S. Army Corps of Engineers and Quartermaster Corps would oversee what would then be a super top-secret facility. My uncles' job in South Carolina wrapped up on schedule, but they were clearly on the map as major players. No more "Hole in the fence" operations for Nilon Brothers Caterers. In their chosen field, the brothers rocked the 50s and 60s.

In 1971 the two brothers still in the business nailed another over-the-moon crown jewel: an exclusive contract to sell all food, drink and novelties in Philadelphia's Veteran's Stadium at the south end of Broad Street near the Old Navy Yard. The contract would last 15 years, a fitting swan song for an incredibly blessed catering career.

Over 50 million Philadelphia sports fans would attend Eagles, Phillies, and Temple University football games, as well as mega concerts and other events at the Vet and JFK Stadium during my uncles' tenure.

As I said: "Tug had a point."

BUSTED

I understand I'm asking a lot from anyone reading this while offering only random verbal "snapshots" about life at the Vet when the lights were turned off, and the fans went home. Stories might help keep this on the playing field and with that thought in mind, a good place to start might be in the very center of the stadium which would be right behind second base.

I will get back to my uncles and specifics about the apartment, but first there's something that occurred about nine months after I moved in. If you're wondering how I got away with living there, I suppose it all came down to this: I made a very deliberate point of having as many people as possible become comfortable seeing me almost anywhere at any time. Becoming ubiquitous made me invisible. I survived my shenanigans in the stadium by adhering to the adage of simply hiding in plain sight. While this story is not a good example of "hiding" very well it does demonstrate how turning up almost anywhere at any time became thoroughly taken for granted.

One incredibly mild midsummer night I came back from J.C. Dobbs Tavern on South Street so hammered, I impulsively wandered into shallow center field, passing out on the AstroTurf behind second base. I went out on the field to lie on my back and look up at a full moon. The Phillies were on the west coast somewhere at the time.

I awoke in an eerie predawn mist, a German Shepherd licking my face. I think the dog's name might have been "Axel," but don't hold me to it. There was a security guard standing over me holding a flashlight.

His first words: "Oh, it's you."

I sat up, scratching Axel behind his ears. He began licking my hand as the guard clicked off his light, laughing, saying, "You seriously can't be out here when 'Chuckles' arrives. If he saw this, it'd be both our asses." He was bang on target. "Chuckles" Harrigan was one of the senior city officials at the Vet. He was ambitious and always out to move up the totem pole. I feared what he'd do if he found out about the apartment. City workers at the Vet didn't call him "Chuckles" behind his back because he was fun to be around. If you had the misfortune of getting on his bad side it could get intense.

I stood up apologizing to the guard for putting him on the spot as he said, "Look, just go wherever it is you go and sleep it off." Neither angry nor exasperated, the guard seemed genuinely relieved that the body on the field was only me. The guard was bemused if anything, looking at me curiously, shaking his head, laughing when he spoke.

I shuffled off towards the apartment in left field, Axel trailing me. The guard made some soft whistling sound. Axel looked at me with big doe eyes, then at the guard, moving almost reluctantly back to his side. Axel and I had a history. I faded into the mist.

A few hours later I crossed Broad Street to get breakfast at a little fast-food joint across from my office by gate D. It was called "The Nineteenth Hole" or some implausible sport's theme name that made little sense. When I washed my hands in the men's room, I was startled to see one half of my face deeply pitted from sleeping on the AstroTurf. I looked as if I had the worst case of acne imaginable, but only on one side of my face. I understood why the kid taking my order had seemed to be eating his face, chewing his lip to keep from laughing at my appearance.

I looked scarred much of the day but took heart knowing I'd dodged a bullet. I ran into a woman I knew. She exploded with laughter. "What the hell happened to you?"

YOU ALWAYS REMEMBER YOUR FIRST

The stadium was always a "Twilight Zone" experience for me, always a surreal place where I felt extreme peace. It certainly didn't start out that way. To fully grasp the wonder that building held for me, you must take a sober look at what happened the first time I ever set foot on the ball field, literally.

My first time in the Vet was bizarre.

The first Phillies game in the new stadium was played on April 10th, 1971. At the time I was a full-time college student at Widener University in Chester, Pennsylvania, while holding down a full-time job on the graveyard shift in the Blade Shop at Westinghouse south of the Airport.

My hyperactive life was like running on a hamster wheel while on steroids, but I'd adjusted to it and as things go, it became normal. It was just my life; what I had to do, and I did it.

When the new ballpark opened, I was in a manic phase, cramming for finals last semester of my senior year. I didn't get down to the stadium until mid-May when my youngest brother, Kevin, invited me to a game. I had graduated magna cum laude on the 10th of May,1971. The pressure was finally off. I was happy to attend a game on a mild late spring evening like any other normal baseball fan. Wasn't going to happen.

As we were wending our way through slowly moving cars in the parking lot, heading towards the stadium, I asked Kevin where our seats were located. He replied we didn't have seats because we didn't have tickets. As the crowd moved towards the stadium, heading up ramps towards the turnstiles on the 300-level, Kevin led me down a truck ramp under Gate H. I've been around Kevin enough to know my youngest brother has a hell of a lot more street smarts than I do. I followed Kevin down the ramp.

A security guard, all business, was having none of it when Kevin tried to talk our way past him. Kevin spotted somebody he knew, the guy interceded, telling the guard we worked for Nilon Brothers. That wasn't good enough either as we didn't have badges. Our guy ran over to the nearby food commissary and came back with Pat Nilon, our cousin. Pat vouched for us. We were in.

The food commissary storage area contained freezer and refrigeration rooms larger than my entire apartment, and the cavernous room also housed a 45-foot long ice-making machine that could easily satisfy the needs of 65,000 fans. I hadn't seen Pat in a while. It was good to catch up with him, but he was under pressure, cool about it but focused. Kevin said he wanted to get out in the stadium because he didn't want to miss the first pitch. We headed over to a down ramp that led out onto right field near the Phillies Bullpen.

A local high school band was coming off the field from pre-game National Anthem activities and marching up the ramp, four abreast, still playing their instruments, coming straight at us.

I'm lovin' it.

I thought we would get out of their way but Kevin says "Follow me" over his shoulder and plunges with no hesitation down the ramp straight into the middle of the band.

I followed him, but not so sure I'm loving it anymore.

We're walking rapidly down ramp between the middle of four rows of the marching band, instruments roaring, as they continue to march in place, game faces still on. The band moves slowly up the incline in the opposite direction. The band never missed a beat, but I've never seen such wide-eyed incredulity as from these kids in that brief passing. Most of the band members and I were equally blown away. I'm certain I looked at them with the same gob smacked expression they had for us. Step by step, I sensed Kevin was leading me into a nasty jackpot. Nothing subtle going on here. This could go bad lots of ways, but I didn't see any way it could go well. Still, I followed him. What was he thinking? Hell's bells! What was I thinking?

By the time we reach the tail end of the band, still out on the field, they had begun marching in place due to some jam-up at the top of the ramp. We broke free of cover; the band still almost twenty yards out into right field. I feel naked and alone under the glare of all the lights, walking into right field in a state-of-the-art coliseum I've never seen before, looking up at maybe 50,000 fans. Everybody is ramped up for a wild night. You can feel an electrical buzz. For extreme sports fans, it's almost like a taser jolt. The excited frenzy leading up to the first pitch can be a great experience, but not if you're out in right field.

The Phillies had taken the field, warming up, lobbing balls around the horn. We're walking single file down the right-field foul line towards first base. I remember an outfielder who, after lobbing a ball into center field, looked at us quizzically, pausing a nano-second in his movement to shrug before turning to snag a ball from the shortstop. His movements were laconic, measured and casual.

The first batter is moving towards the plate. I'm following Kevin down the sideline feeling like I'm about to throw up in front of thousands of strangers. Only a few feet from the foul line, I know we're more than a little out of bounds. I'm pissing myself. I hadn't signed on for any of this. I just thought it would be a hot dog and a beer at the old ball game. Now I'm thinking hand cuffs and bail money.

When the stadium first opened, the Phillies had two picnic areas on the same level as the playing field just past the dugouts. The picnic area was a great idea and an incredible way to experience a ballgame. Various organizations: scouts, church groups, whatever, could purchase a certain minimum number of tickets and bring their own picnic lunches into the area. There were picnic tables scattered about in these areas, which were completely covered with AstroTurf. You could wander around the picnic area or stand at the very edge of the playing field, watching the game while leaning on the three-foot high fence that separated the picnickers from what players called "The Show." It's almost as though you were in the dugout. You are right beside the dugout, only a few yards farther down the baseline. The area also had bleacher seats, mini bleacher seats really, maybe only seven or eight rows high and thirty-five feet wide. Anybody who ever enjoyed a game in the picnic area knows it was the greatest way to see a ball game.

The pitcher and the batter are staring each other down. Kevin and I are standing on the wrong side of a gate into the picnic area. A security guard behind the gate stares at us in panic.

Kevin surprises me again, hollering, "Open the gate! Game's about to start."

The guard yelling above the roaring crowd echoes my brother. "Game's about to start, hurry up, get in here!" He opens the gate. We walk in nodding like we all accomplished something good.

Kevin fist bumps the guard's shoulder in that guy way.

We move through the picnic area to one of the area's small bleachers. You'd think Kevin owned the place. Nobody seems to look at us or even realizes we exist. All eyes are on the field. We climb to the top row of the little bleachers, settling in.

Great seats.

Game's underway, no one challenged us, everything's cool. I turn to Kevin. "What the hell was that all about"!

With his eyes riveted on the batter Kevin says, "If you're out on the field, nobody's ever going to question you. They don't know you, but they know you must be connected somehow. You've gotta be 'Somebody' if you're out there walking around the field." He looked around smiling. "Great seats, huh?"

Crack of the bat launches a long ball. It arches into left field towards the foul ball pole sucking all the air out of the fans. Too close to call for a hanging moment, then running foul, bouncing hard off the walkway, ricocheting up into section 354.

I couldn't know it at the time, but eight years later I would be living in a Secret Apartment under those same seats beneath the exact spot where I saw fans scrambling for the ball.

And so it went, my first encounter in the new stadium casting a long shadow over my future, a harbinger of something far beyond my wildest imagination. The die was cast.

A VET TURNED LOOSE IN THE VET

By the mid-1970s, I was the person in my extended family dancing to music nobody else could hear. I'd given up a college deferment in 1965 and enlisted in the Army: "Airborne, Vietnam, Unassigned." This meant the Army was contractually obligated to send me to Vietnam, but only in an airborne unit. What specific role they would have me fulfill I left to their discretion. Years later a woman I dated briefly after I got out of the Army asked me, "What were you thinking?" I didn't have any way of answering her.

I didn't get physically injured in Vietnam in any way you could measure, but those closest to me sensed something intangibly different when I came home. My closest friends were new friends, people I met after the Army who had no frame of reference as to my personality before and after. They had no history with me and were not disconcerted by any changes. Some old friends drifted away. To be fair, they came by their discomfort honestly. They didn't know me anymore, but it was equally true I didn't know myself. I remember my Uncle Bob, who served in the artillery on New Guinea during World War II, emphatically warning me: "In the Army, never, ever, volunteer for anything."

When I enlisted in the Army, I volunteered for everything. I signed on for the wild ride.

After a few years of intensive training, Infantry Officer

Candidate School and some more volunteering, I ended up as a 25-year-old 1st Lieutenant, the Commanding Officer of a Special Forces A-team, Operational Detachment A-231 in the South-Central Highlands. Our little outpost ringed only by rusty coils of barbed wire sat less than a hard day's march from the Cambodian border on seriously dangerous ground. Marching the same distance due north of our camp would place you in the Ia drang Valley near Landing Zone X-ray. The largest battle and loss of American lives in the war had taken place there a few years earlier. It would remain the most catastrophic confrontation for the entire war. America lost over 304 men in a little over 72 hours. Mel Gibson's movie, based on Joe Galloway's excellent book, both sharing the same title, We Were Soldiers, depicts this battle. My Special Forces A-Team, at Tieu Atar, lived and ran border ops just south of The Ia Drang Valley. In mid-November,1965, more than three thousand Americans took part in that fight with two full-strength air mobile battalions on the ground, with artillery support sling loaded into the area and awesome amounts of helicopter and fixed-wing air power. B-52s stacked in thousand-foot intervals from 17,000 to 33,000 feet circled ominously, ready to drop 2000 pound bombs on call.

Two years later, in 1967, long range recon teams and electronic surveillance operations indicated increasing enemy activity on the southern side of the Chu Pong Massif. My camp was built there to plug the gap. I ran operations there with Fred Henry in the summer of 1968. Two US Special Forces soldiers would go out with about fifty poorly trained and insufficiently armed Montagnards, the Stone Age mountain men guys in Special Forces came to love. I certainly fell in love with them. You couldn't help yourself. Unlike the disastrous battle that had taken place on the other side of the mountain just north of our camp, Tieu Atar never had any artillery or laid on air support and we were damned lucky to survive some extremely lopsided encounters. Most of the men I knew on the A-teams did their jobs to the best of their ability, taking their chances for granted. It may seem insane to anyone who didn't live on the border, but most of us became blasé about living on the edge. To us, it was simply what we were asked to do. The full title of Galloway's book offers some insight to this: We Were Soldiers Once, and Young.

Coming home physically intact was good enough for me, but I was missing the point. Like many Vets I had issues I never dealt with because when I first came home I kept myself so hyper-busy I didn't have time to think or let myself feel how the miasma of war had crawled inside my head, made a nest and fouled it. Within eight days of coming home I'd returned to college full time as a day student while also working midnight to 8 a.m. six days a week in the blade shop at Westinghouse just below the airport. After graduation I didn't use my degree or pursue grad school right away because I wanted to write but took on a second full-time job during the day working with emotionally disturbed children at Elwyn Institute near Media, Pennsylvania. In a way, they were like my Montagnards because they had no guile and were innocent, pure and vulnerable. The kids at Elwyn crawled inside my heart and made a nest but filled it with laughter and unconditional love, a gentle restorative antidote to nightmarish memories of carnage on the Cambodian Border.

Thirty years later, a psychiatric nurse at The VA Hospital in Philadelphia would tell me I was a poster child for Post-Traumatic Stress Disorder. She thought my love for and involvement with the children were a self-administered palliative for the chaos and frustration I had at the time.

By 1976 the wheels seemed to come off my little red wagon with growing mixed reviews about my stability and state of mind. Nothing I wrote about Vietnam satisfied me in any way. I couldn't describe my feelings in words. I could never get it right. I tracked down and began communicating with a handful of grievously suffering mothers of friends damaged forever by the loss of their sons in our debacle in Southeast Asia. Through cards, letters and phone calls we became close friends, and I realized they demanded of me something they never put into words. I never fully understood this at the time, and it only came to me after all of them had passed on. These women, every one of them, to their very last breath, never got over the loss of their children. I came to know in a profound way their need was for me to simply explain their children were just boys who simply loved their families and country and felt obligated to serve in some way when their country told them we were justifiably at war. When our country asked their sons to serve and protect, they stepped forward. I didn't have to explain the war. I wasn't even to try. I had to tell their children's stories in a humane way while not romanticizing the notion, going to war proves you're a man. Nothing I wrote ever measured up to what these women needed from me. I was a pathetic Don Quixote tilting at windmills, trying to find words and images that could simply tell why their boys had gone off to a war so many Americans came to despise. Unfulfilled, I was spinning in a never-ending downward spiral.

I may have been harmless to others, but I was clearly a loss to myself. I dated some incredible women, but they were great sparks to wet tinder. No matter how open or loving, it always came to their realizing I was no one with whom they could ever feather a nest. Relationships never went anywhere good for very long.

My circling the drain of dead-end jobs eventually led to working in the parking lots at the stadium. My cousin Terry oversaw all parking operations at the Sports Complex. Terry's responsibilities were a big job in every way but remained a poor stepchild when compared to the excitement of working on the inside at Phillies and Eagles Games. Working the lots was also laboriously exhausting as parking operations covered every event at the Spectrum across the street and mega concerts at the JFK Memorial Stadium. That old girl, built in 1926, could hold 120,000 for concerts but hadn't aged well. Our family had emotional connections with JFK, as their earliest and largest catering events occurred there starting with the Army-Navy games in 1950. Many cousins and I had worked there handing out box lunches in the press box since we were eight years old.

Years later when JFK imploded to make room for what is currently the Wells Fargo Center it was, for me, like having to put a beloved pet to sleep because its existence had become nothing but bone-suffering pain.

Parking operations at the Stadium Complex were a separate contract with the city from their food and novelty concessions. Parking had not been any part of Nilon Brothers' responsibilities when the stadium opened in 1971. As I said, my uncles ran all food and novelty operations during events at the stadium. That was it, and that was more than enough. They worked their way up to this all their lives and they would finish their careers on a high note.

Parking came later, and it came suddenly without warning. Something critically untoward happened less than two weeks before the Phillies season opener in the spring of 1977. Whatever happened required drastic measures. I never knew why, but Joel Ralph, The Commissioner of Parks and Recreation for The South Philadelphia Sports Complex, was forced to summarily cancel the existing parking operations contract. Everybody at the Vet knew, respected and loved Commissioner Ralph who had his offices on level four of the Vet next to the Eagles Offices. Joel was always around the building and knew Bob Nilon well and Bob's well-established reputation parking at events as large as Army-Navy Games since 1950. Joel approached my Uncle Bob asking him if he could take over the remainder of the parking contract, which would run until 1982. A "no brainer," Bob jumped in. Unlike my uncles' Vet contract for concessions, Nilon Brothers were now involved in running parking operations for every event held at all three buildings comprising the Sports Complex.

Bob tapped his son Terry, "TJ", to run parking operations. TJ threw a crew together and offered me work as a cashier/supervisor at one of the main gates on the north lot which surrounded the stadium. Out of work with nothing going for me, I gratefully said yes.

Running the lots was constantly onerous. Terry oversaw almost three hundred and sixty-five events a year. There were only rare days when all three venues were dark. He was also responsible for cleaning the lots after events and in winter, all snow removal. It wasn't any kind of work schedule and responsibility I wanted. There were many double-event days and even some triple-event days. The highest number of events held in the three venues were always hosted at the Spectrum, averaging over 220 events annually. The Vet was next in line with all Phillies, Eagles and Temple University home and playoff games as well as other major events. The largest crowd capacity events in the Complex were always "sold out" mega-concerts at JFK, topping out at 120,000 plus capacities. Terry also ran off-site parking gigs at The Mann Music Center in Fairmount Park, as well as all soccer and football games at the Navy-Marine Memorial Stadium in Annapolis and occasional golf tournaments such as the U.S. Open and The Westchester Classic. If the Phillies were in town at the same time as concerts at the Spectrum and Mann Music Center, Terry had three-event days. It could be, and often was, razor's edge insane. There was almost never a break in the action.

I was content being an occasional cashier supervisor, working only when I wanted, making my own schedule. I wouldn't want Terry's responsibilities for anything. Living in Chester in an old Victorian house just off Widener's Campus, I'd ride my bike 10 miles up Interstate 95 to the stadium, copping a ride home at night with my buddy Clem, a friend on the crew with a pickup truck. Work was plentiful and I could get all the events I wanted with the freedom to come and go as I pleased. It suited my aimless lifestyle, and I settled in and became comfortable.

I never looked ahead nor thought about the future.

Terry however had bigger plans. For him, the parking operation was a thankless meat grinder in deplorable weather conditions with no wiggle room for a normal life. When everything ran smoothly it wasn't anything, he got credit for, but when things blew up, as they easily could, he was on the carpet. Cleaning the lots after an Eagles Game could be a nightmare, as this was back in the days when there were no restrictions on tailgating. The lots surrounding the stadium after an Eagles Game recalled images of the ruins outside the walls of a medieval city sacked by a Mongolian hoard.

Terry was right, Parking was a dead-end job, and he was wrapped too tightly for the insane nutso schedule and "free-fire zone" atmosphere in the lots. Terry came up with a novel exit plan. I must admit it was sheer unalloyed genius. TJ's vision was to open Nilon's Sports World, a sports novelty store on the Wildwood by-the- sea Boardwalk in New Jersey. Working a little over four months in the summer, Terry would sell quality replica jerseys and every type of sports paraphernalia imaginable. Off season he could kick back and follow the sun.

Terry tapped into his father's well-established line of credit and the clout of Nilon's insanely high-volume novelty purchases at the Vet as well as their discount rate and used it to stock his operation at the seashore. He also negotiated an unheard of "90-day net." Terry did not have to pay for any of his stock until after he had it for 90 days from time of delivery. At the end of the season, as if this wasn't the sweetheart deal of the century already, Terry could return all unused merchandise. The following summer Nilon's Sports World was able to offer all of the newest styles of jerseys, hats, and God knows what sports merchandise available for every team, in every sport, and he didn't have to make his first payment until mid-August. It was pure entrepreneurial genius. Terry couldn't lose, but there was one major problem.

"TJ the DJ" couldn't leave for the land of sandy beaches and nubile women unless he found someone to take his place running parking. No one else in either of my uncles' families would even consider working in the lots, a poor stepchild to the big action on the inside. I was family in some ways but not in others, primarily when it came to money. I never thought about managing the lots because it didn't interest me. I knew what the role demanded and never thought they would offer it to me.

I had just taken a few tokes on a one hitter as I sat meditating in the Phillies dugout one Friday afternoon when the hammer came down on my free-wheeling lifestyle. I never saw it coming. It was five weeks before the season opener and The Phillies were down in Clearwater not quite holding their own in spring training's "Grapefruit League." Not too many workers were in the stadium. The Spectrum was dark that night. I was in the stadium picking up my paycheck before heading uptown on the subway to meet some friends at Dobbs for some mischief on South Street. In my mind, I was already there when I walked the foul line into right field to the ramp near the Phillies bullpen. Heading down the underground hallway, I ran into my Uncle Jack. He was coming towards me with his perpetual "You don't want to fuck with me" frown that always seemed to give him an edge with anybody he met. Jack wasn't a big man, but he'd mastered a signature defensive expression, sort of a sneer but hard to place. It made you uncomfortable and more than not, people not only didn't take Jack on but preferred to stay out of his way altogether. His disarming edge on this occasion threw me so far off base I never recovered till after he walked away.

Jack broke into an uncharacteristically pleasant grin when he saw me. In my feathered state of mind, I panicked, jumping to the conclusion I must have screwed something up big time to put so much bounce in his step. Jack looked almost happy.

"I hear you're taking over the parking operation" he said with a smile that made me wonder if that smoke a friend had given me had been laced with embalming fluid. I can't remember what I said, but it must have given Jack the impression I knew what he was talking about and was excited and looking forward to the opportunity they were giving me. I felt like Eddie Haskell on the old television show, "Leave it to Beaver." I babbled. I gushed nonsense.

What I was thinking as I groveled, was running the parking lot might be the last thing I ever wanted to do. We spoke amicably for a few minutes and Jack assured me I was fully capable of running the lots and he had full confidence in me. That could only mean he had no short- term viable options.

I thanked my uncle, and we both pretended we had somewhere we had to rush off to as we headed our separate ways. I forgot to get my paycheck and wandered in a daze up to the parking ops office looking for Terry as I figured how to "Jimmy Hoffa" his body. TJ wasn't anywhere to be found, and that was probably for the best. I ended up at the far end of the bar at Dobbs. Donny left a bottle of Irish whiskey in front of me as we reassessed the whole thing.

Some friends and the Jameson convinced me the job might not be a bad thing after all. I would have my own key to a very obscure door on the far side of the stadium, and all my friends would have season tickets to all the Phillies and Eagles home games.

What could possibly go wrong with that?

DA BONES

Before we go any further, I have to give you some insight as to what the bones of the apartment were like. There were never any photos taken of the Secret Apartment, as I was afraid of who might get their hands on them and where that could lead. On this one issue of security I was maniacal, and this was the era before everyone had cell phones with cameras. I can tell you with certainty photographs never happened.

Location: The apartment was in left field under the slope of the 300-level seats, section 354, and the only door into the apartment was on the 200-level concourse on the left side of the alcove that led out to the seats. The door was marked 2-65. If you were on the 200-level and walked out through the alcove to stand at the railing looking down, you would be above the visiting team's bullpen, the foul ball pole just to your right.

The physical size of the apartment was the exact size allocated to any rest rooms or concession stands on the 200-level, meaning the room occupied all the area under the 300-level seats from one alcove passageway opening out onto the playing field extending as far as the next alcove over. I don't have any existing blueprints, but I'm estimating the area which had once been intended to be a novelty stand to have been about 60 feet long to roughly 30-something feet wide. By "Wide" I'm referring to the wall opening onto the interior concourse where fans would approach the counter to purchase novelties and extending back from the counter as far as the much lower rear wall, which would be the wall closest to the playing field. In the case of my apartment, these two service windows were always permanently closed and padlocked on the inside. In every concession stand, the ceiling above the service counters was roughly 16-feet high and sloped towards the field on the same grade as the 300-level seats above. The interior wall closest to the field was just under 5 feet. In any one of these spaces between the alcoves, if utilized as a men's room, this interior wall would be the low wall where the bank of urinals were located. In a ladies room, this wall closest to the field would be a row of sinks. In my apartment, I placed the head of my bed against that wall.

If the solid steel door was open and you looked into the room, you wouldn't see anything of interest. The only thing visible was a long corridor of cardboard boxes on both sides, maybe 7 feet wide which appeared to lead to a dead end, a literal "box canyon," about 40 feet into the room. The room appeared to be nothing, but a storage area filled entirely with cardboard boxes of parking tickets for events stacked about 7-feet high. What you couldn't see unless you walked to the far end of the aisle was that there was a hidden opening to the right that led to a double-blind before opening into my living area. There was nothing to catch anyone's interest from the doorway. Anyone looking into the room when the door was open wouldn't see or suspect the unauthorized apartment hidden behind box walls.

In the living area, which was almost one half of the entire area, the concrete floor was covered with new AstroTurf. The city had resurfaced the entire playing field in the last year. I had access to the surplus AstroTurf. Beneath my new AstroTurf, I'd added additional foam padding, so the floor was softer and much more comfortable than the playing field. Great flooring for a man cave.

The apartment was furnished with everything most guys would need or want in any other apartment with few exceptions as I had been using the room to store the furniture of a Philadelphia Eagle who had gotten nervous about signing a new lease on his apartment before camp opened at West Chester in July, 1979. He had a bad feeling that a new coach hired in the spring of that year might not have plans to keep him around, no matter how well he excelled in camp. His vibes were right on. His teammates agreed he had one of his best camps ever and couldn't understand why he got cut from the squad.

The apartment was predominantly furnished with things he left behind, and he left everything.

Centered in the dramatically spacious high ceiling area sat a large Ethan Allen coffee table shaped like a gear that turned like a Lazy-Susan. Around the table I'd placed several overstuffed chairs, a few colorful director's chairs, a giant purple beanbag chair, and a daybed-like sofa. There was a kitchen area with an oversized stainless-steel tub with hot and cold running water left over from the room's short-lived days as a novelty concession stand. A long room-dividing waist-high counter topped with a Mr. Coffee, toaster oven, grilling hotplate, stereo and turntable sat adjacent to a full-sized refrigerator, giving me everything needed to survive in "Hamburger Country." A pair of thirty inch Kenwood Speakers I shipped home from Vietnam were on both sides of my conversation pit and I placed the head of my double bed against the lowest wall, closest to the playing field which was only about four and a half feet high. I could sit up in bed and not bump my head but easily reach the wall phone mounted nearby.

Beside the bed I placed a large overstuffed chair with an ottoman and a table with a reading lamp that serviced reading either in bed or in the chair.

Vet Stadium had its own 3 digit phone directory and phones

were located in every concession stand, locker room, or office in the stadium and could receive calls from outside the building as long as the incoming call came through the switchboard at City Hall at MUnicipal 6-1776. My extension was x-217. I had access to a sink and toilet in a powder room in my office on the other side of the 200-level concourse in the outer rim of the stadium. I had regular phones in my office also. A door in the outer wall of the Vet in the truck bay next to my office in the outer rim allowed me to enter or leave the stadium at will. The Phillies, Sixers and at least one city office were also situated in this more than sixty-foot wide outer rim. In the truck bay, I kept a golf cart which resembled a miniature metallic green pickup truck. It had an enclosed cab and one bench seat large enough for three people in an uncomfortable squeeze. There were no doors and like a pickup, there was a small truck bed with lacquered wood panels on the sides.

The golf cart-like truck was for running around the lots, but I'd ventured outside the stadium as far afield as Lou's Deli tucked in the middle of the primary loading platform at the Food Distribution Center five blocks east. What an incredible location for a deli. The loading dock where eighteen wheelers backed in bringing the bulk of all fresh food to Philadelphia was dangerously abuzz with forklifts teetering with pallets of food, zipping about in a beehive of activity. Moving around the loading dock you had to be studiously alert, step lively and be on your game. Depending on the time of year and which sports teams were in season, you might find booths in the deli crammed with several Philadelphia ballplayers, coaches, or front office people. I drove my tricked-out golf cart to the food distribution area, always staying on the sidewalk. I also made it to several bars and restaurants on Packer Avenue. The police never bothered me. Hey, it's South Philly.

I could also drive my golf cart anywhere in the stadium at any time. A brown pickup truck came with the job, and I kept it inside the Vet in the large truck bay outside my office. Getting around inside the building I had my 10-speed bike and an incredible pair of professional grade street roller skates belonging to the Samoan linebacker, Terry Tautolo, which I used to romp all over the building at all hours. It may not have occurred to a lot of sports fans attending events, but the Vet turned out to be one of the greatest skate parks conceivable. Skating the Vet was a blast.

If I needed a shower, I could head underground to the 100 level where just up the ramp coming off right field next to the Phillies bullpen was a locker room with showers for city workers. I kept two lockers there, one with workout gear, flip-flops and toiletries and another beside it with clean towels and several changes of clothes. There were many more lockers than the demand for them, and the locker room was accessible to me 24/7.

For laundry I had access to the industrial sized washer and dryer in the commissary. I had a key to the commissary and during my time at the Vet I ate a lot of hotdogs.

There were a few occasions when I took an air mattress, poncho and poncho liner and slept under the stars on the walkway atop the 700-level walkway. It was a hoot.

My Secret Apartment was a "guy thing" to be sure, the quintessential man cave and no place to raise a family, but I was single, had issues I never dealt with, and was maybe more than a little nuts. Living in the Vet satisfied everything I wanted or needed at that point in my life. The apartment was as cozy and comfortable as could be with the mind blowing off the chart advantage of having the Phillies and Eagles playing their home games 40 feet from what I considered to be my front door.

I went to bed one night in June 1980, during a rain delay and woke up to catch the end of the game in my bathrobe after 3 am. The only question anybody asked me was not why I was standing there in a bathrobe and flip flops, but where did I get the hot coffee

I was drinking as all the concession stands had closed hours ago.

BEFORE HE DIES

One of my favorite stories from time at the Vet involved a friend, John McManus, a bartender who lived up in Fairmount and had a Ph.D. from Syracuse. Johnny had a secret second life. Occasionally he would disappear, having hopped on a bus up to McGill University in Montreal where he would co-author books with Charlie Laughlin, a faculty member. Charlie hailed from Texas and had been an item with Janis Joplin way back in the day, long before either of them became cult figures in their destined fields. Charlie and the full tilt mezzo-soprano had a battered old white van they lived in and his CB handle on the road was "Texas Crude." I would have paid anything to have caught their act together.

I never fully understood much about John and Charlie's esoteric topics such as "Biogenetic Structuralism" but knew the two of them well enough to know their "BS" was seriously respected in academic circles and John McManus is still being quoted as far away as Western Australia. John tended bar at The London, Rembrandt's and the upstairs bar at the TLA on South Street. He was a good drinking buddy and had gotten his degree from Syracuse. John was simply happy being a bartender. It suited his Tom Waits, hard drinking, black coffee and chain-smoking lifestyle. The expression "Lost Weekend" comes to mind. One of his longtime, on again, off again girlfriends was known as "The Fog." I

TOM GARVEY

thought it just a really a clever nickname for her until I saw her driver's license. Fog was her last name.

In the blue haze of cigarette smoke just before last call at Dobb's I ran into a mutual friend and local musician and songwriter, the multi-talented Skip Denenberg, who's shared the stage with the likes of Willie Nelson, Warren Zevon and The Neville Brothers. Skip's got chops. He asked me if I had seen Johnny lately. It had been awhile, and he told me I should give John a call 'cause he heard McManus' dad was losing a battle with some insidious cancer. John's alma mater, Syracuse, scheduled to crush Temple at the Vet the coming Saturday, gave me a possible opportunity to lift his spirits for a few hours.

I called John and told him Syracuse was coming to town and maybe we could get together for a few beers, hot dogs and catch the game together. John told me about his father, but not in the way I thought he would. He was laughing.

"This is incredible. My father's losing a battle to cancer. Just last week he tells me there is one thing I got to do for him before he dies. He is football nuts. Syracuse football nuts! Says they have this little running back, Morris, and he wants me to see him because he thinks he might become Syracuse's greatest running back, ever. Can you believe this would be my father's dying wish?" He went on to tell me again about how fanatical his dad was about Syracuse Football. He didn't have to. McManus had me at "Dying wish."

I told McManus I'd be out on the lots before the game, but I'd plan to be free before kickoff and to meet me at my office. We could catch a beer at the apartment before the game. John showed up 20 minutes before the game. It was a beautiful mid-September, Indian summer afternoon, and I was in the office working on schedules for upcoming events, the oversized garage bay door was open when he walked in. Setting aside my paperwork, we headed across the inner concourse to the apartment. John dug a couple of beers out of the refrigerator while I put a Pink Floyd LP on the stereo. We sat down around the large gear-shaped coffee table that turned like a lazy-Susan and torched a joint. I was pleased Denenberg tipped me off to John's dad's situation and that the timing was right for us to link up for the game.

John told his father he was going to the game. That he would see Jim Morris run. His father was right about Morris, who would one day hold 19 New York Giants' franchise records and be a key factor in their 1986 Super Bowl victory. John's father sensed Morris was destined for greatness and was over the top about John seeing him in action. He kept shaking his head and laughing. "You can't believe what my going to this game means to my father."

The roar of the crowd brought us back to what was going on outside. We poured our beers into blue paper cups with the large white "N" on them and headed out into the stands to find seats before kickoff. Within ten minutes it became obvious that if Temple was a seventeen-point underdog at home, nobody told them. The Vet was their house, and the "Owls" were up for a fight. They shut Morris down. At halftime Temple led by double digits, Morris held to thirteen yards total offense. John and I headed back to the Secret Apartment and that's when things got weird.

Everybody knows someone from their college days so self-destructive you never thought they would live to see thirty. For John, that guy was Jay Haight. Jay even had a tattoo: "Till death do we party." I saw a wildman barreling towards us, oblivious to the crowd, bouncing off walls and people like a pinball. Nobody you would want to get anywhere near if you could avoid him, I didn't realize this was the guy I'd heard outrageous stories about.

John told me that Jay had been pulled over once after a Grateful Dead Concert on The New York Thruway after going through a speed trap. Jay was tanked on Tequila, hash and acid at the time. The state trooper asked Jay if he had any idea how fast he'd been going. Jay lied spontaneously, tossing out a guess a few miles over the speed limit, humbly apologetic, promising he'd be more careful, begging for a break. Abject apologies weren't going to save him. The state bulls knew they had a live one on the hook. Jay had been clocked at 24 miles an hour.

The cop noted Jay's license required him to wear glasses while driving. Jay told the officers he had a prescription windshield, then threw up on their shoes.

Jay did not make it home that night.

McManus had lost contact with Jay but thought he was probably dead. John had not seen Jay yet, and I did not know the amusing man without a shirt, his entire torso and face painted day glow orange, was the infamous Jay Haight. Jay did not know what city or state he was in or planet he was on.

McManus and I were about to slip into the apartment. John and Jay spotted each other at the same time, and they were screaming, jumping up and down and hugging each other as they hadn't seen each other in over ten years. Whatever Jay's orange coloring was, it was all over McManus. It made Jay look like he was melting.

When they calmed down a bit, we came to understand Jay and some Syracuse friends had an old school bus painted orange with a keg in the back. They attended all home games and any away games within a reasonable driving distance. Somewhere out in the Stadium there was a busload of orange-painted bodies running loose.

We stood in the alcove, the two of them overjoyed to have run in to each other. John asked Jay if he would like to smoke a joint. Jay looked around the crowded alcove conspiratorially, wondering if it was cool to do it there. He had no monitor and I think he might have lit up right there if John hadn't said, "No, come with us. Tommy has an apartment."

Jay followed us as I unlocked the unmarked door and led him inside as if it were the most natural thing in the world. We went down the little hallway made by the towering maze of cardboard boxes and led Jay around the double blind into my hidden living area with AstroTurf flooring, gear shaped coffee table, chairs, stereo and everything. I got a round of long neck Rolling Rocks out of the fridge while John put something on the stereo as we hunkered down around the coffee table. The artificial fireplace nearby cast a warm glow across the area. It was homey, comfortable, cozy. Jay did not seem fazed by any of this or aware anything was unusual. I did not think he knew where he was or even cared.

I watched John, fully relaxed, enjoying himself in the company of an old friend. Jay, totally oblivious to where he was or how he'd gotten there, was having one hell of a good time. Jerry Garcia's "Casey Jones" in the background.

Another joint and another round of beers, until we were interrupted by an incredibly loud noise. It made us stop a moment and look around. The crowd was getting psyched up for the second half kick-off, stomping their feet on the sloping ceiling above, but for all Jay seemed aware of, we could have been on the moon. John muttered something about us getting back into the stands and we all began to stand up.

Jay stood up halfway, then froze.

He looked around, distraught, fear in his eyes. He went down slowly, collapsing in his chair, making a sound like air escaping from a balloon. His eyes grew larger as he looked around warily, as if for the very first time sensing he was somewhere far out of bounds, out of his comfort zone without a clue.

"Where are we?" he asked, panic in his voice. His jumble of questions ran into each other. "How did we get here? Did we leave the stadium? Is it okay to be here?" There was genuine fear in his eyes as if once again, he had crossed some boundary he couldn't control when he drank too much and took drugs. His eyes darted everywhere, craning his neck, looking everywhere, taking everything in, as if for the first time, and unable to figure anything out. I thought he might cry.

John reassured Jay in a soothing voice, "Everything's cool." There would not be any trouble or problems with us being in the apartment. Jay kept looking around everywhere as if he were seeing it all for the first time and could not make sense of anything.

This man had stood at the end of the plank before.

When he spoke, what Jay Haight said drove home everything I had ever heard about him and remains one of the sadder things I have ever heard from someone at the frayed end of reality.

Jay spoke as if he were a frightened little child.

"Where are we that I can explain where you took me, so they won't think I'm just crazy?"

It wasn't only his words that made me feel for him. He looked off into space, seeing something he feared, something he should fear. The tone of his voice held sadness, maybe defeat, despair, or maybe a sense he'd never be able to explain some of the places he went in his mind. I saw a man who had come to a point where he didn't trust himself anymore.

I realized sadly that Jay had come back to his friends, maybe too many times, from places that he could not explain because they might not exist. It was not that his friends might think he was crazy. It was to himself that Jay had to explain where he was. His grasp of reality was fragile, something he didn't own.

John laughed, reassuring Jay we would come to where his buddies were sitting with some beers and explain everything. Jay told us where he thought they were, as best he could, and we left the secret apartment fully intending to link up with some hotdogs and beers.

When I locked the door behind us Jay turned and looked at it as though he had come through some black hole through which he could never return. He wandered into the crowd mumbling something about the men's room, and that was the last I ever saw of him.

Jay's description of where his gang was sitting didn't pan out. How difficult could it be to locate dozens of half-naked, fully drunk men painted orange on a glorious sunny September Saturday afternoon? Wandering the 200 and 300-level seats for too much of the third quarter almost made me begin to wonder if we'd really ever run into Jay Haight and I felt sorry imagining him as he tried to describe where in his muddled world he had gone when he left them to find the men's room. Jay's question haunted me. "How can I tell them where I was, so they won't think I'm just crazy?"

We abandoned our fruitless search for Syracuse's version of The Merry Pranksters, drank our beers, and gave our hot dogs to a family sitting nearby. I fantasized how insane Jay's explaining of his misadventure on his way to the bathroom would sound to old friends who knew his history of breakdancing on the razor's edge.

Jim Morris finally scored a touchdown late in the fourth quarter. That was all Temple gave him, and it wasn't enough. Temple crushed Syracuse 49 to 17. Two weeks later I heard John went back to Syracuse for his father's funeral.

But that wasn't the end of it.

I didn't see Johnny for at least six weeks until I ran into him at the upstairs bar at Dobbs. John saw me, started laughing hysterically, talking so fast and incoherently I couldn't follow him. When McManus told stories he'd sometimes get so excited he mumbled. It was as if he was speaking in a code; using sounds, not syllables. You had to calm him down to understand what he was trying to say. This was one of those times.

What John was trying to say was not just that his dad had died. I told him I had heard about this and offered condolences. John told me he had gone home for the funeral. Friends had taken him out to the legendary off-campus bar "The Big Orange" to tie one on. He'd done some bartending there while a graduate student. Larry Csonka had worked the door as a bouncer at the time, later winning back-to-back Super Bowls with the Miami Dolphins. His contributions to their perfect 1972 season guaranteed Csonka a coveted place in the National Football League's Hall of Fame.

John sobered for a moment. He spoke slowly. What I had taken for hysterical grief seemed more like a confession of guilt. If anything, it was remorse.

"Cruelest thing I've ever done! Ever! Happened at The Big Orange, just before last call." John told me that, after ordering a double for last call, in a haze of cigarette smoke floating above the bar, John spotted Jay Haight across the room. Jay must've seen John at the same time. Jay let out a scream that turned heads, silenced conversations, then began swimming through the crowd, dragging everybody with him like Haley's Comet, pushing and shoving people out of his way, spilling drinks. Impervious to a roar of indignation in his wake, Jay clearly was on a mission. Oblivious to anybody or anything, Jay did not give a rat's ass.

Jay lunged at John, grabbing his shirt with both hands, a drowning man who couldn't swim, screaming "Tell them...tell them it's true.... tell them about the place in Philly...." The entire bar had gone silent, listening.

That's when haphazard male ball busting came into play.

McManus, looking bewildered, shaking his head, looked into Jay's bleary blue eyes.

"Jesus Jay, you look great. I haven't seen you...in what...what is it? 10 years?"

The second McManus said this, he knew he'd gone too far. But before John could come clean, he witnessed one of the most sadly pathetic breakdowns he'd ever seen. He saw an old friend melting into himself. It was a nowhere-else-to-go moment for Jay. He seemed to let go of the string that held the little red balloon filled with all he had left.

John looked at the guys surrounding Jay. None of them seemed surprised in any way. They'd heard stories about the rabbit hole Jay claimed to have fallen down somewhere in that stadium in Philly. Jay was known to embellish his stories with keen colorful details, almost as if they had actually happened, so his friends never knew what to believe. They never could tell but usually defaulted to disbelief. Some of the crowd this night had been orange-colored passengers on that bus trip. Versions, many versions of the story had become local bar legends. Some swayed to believe it because of their need for whimsy and the raw truth Jay sometimes exuded telling his stories. Truth, however strange, has this weird ring to it. It is hard to put into words, but it just sounds right. No words can ever describe it. It is just truth. With Jay, you never knew.

But this was Jay Haight. The good time party guy everybody loved, but nobody wanted to be. Clocked under thirty miles per hour by some no-nonsense state bulls on the New York Thru Way while under the influence of everything but common sense. That Jay Haight, "rabbit hole in Philly" Jay.

Jay dropped to his knees, sitting back on the floor, tears in his eyes.

McManus back peddled as quickly as possible, bailing Jay out and explaining what really happened in Philly and that Jay was telling the truth. Cackling, laughing hysterically and making sounds that fit no alphabet, anywhere, ever, John related the events of his drunken reunion with Jay Haight at The Orange.

Conversations with McManus were a trip.

A lot of alcohol was consumed at The Orange that night after the doors were locked. The good feelings spilled out onto the streets, and John followed Jay's crowd to an after-hours club. They pushed back at the night for the best reason to be in a bar in the first place, storytelling. Jay's story now had new legs, and it ran with the night till the sun came up.

If ball busting were an Olympic Sport, McManus could have gotten a gold medal that night.

TWO ABSURDLY INCONGRUENT EVENTS

The Secret Apartment came about primarily because of two absurdly incongruous events. I'd bet my life that absolutely no one reading this could ever imagine what they might be or their connection.

I'll concede this is one more nonsensical notion from me, but when you latch onto not only what did occur, but also intersected, you'll come to agree I hadn't risked my life at all when I made the bet.

Here goes:

1. Dick Vermeil hired a new assistant coach.

2. The Pope came to town.

Vermeil's new coach was out to show he had something to contribute to the team and spent a lot of time looking at game films scrutinizing players he'd inherited. Nobody's job was safe. Everybody was on the chopping block. He'd played the game himself and coached at the college level but it's not easy to improve the play of guys who had been standouts in a game they'd been dominating since they were eight years old and were now excelling at as professionals. In the coach's defense, the jump from coaching college kids to seasoned pros is a big one, especially when you've never played at that level. And this was his first season on top of the mountain.

One of the locker room jokes about the new coach was that after studying old game films he insisted one of his players could improve his speed at the snap if he completely reversed his stance at the line of scrimmage. This Eagle had been a standout and comfortable with his old stance since the first time he put on a helmet. He wasn't adapting well with the change and realized his chances of making the squad were circling the drain. It didn't help that his new coach seemed overly interested in prying into this free-spirited guy's off the field's social life. He was a normal young man in his prime living the good life of a high-profile sport's celebrity in a city that worshipped their Eagles. That alone gave our Eagle good reason to be nervous about a new coach scrutinizing his off the field activities.

For the purpose of this story let's say this Eagle's name was "Ozzie" and the fact that the Eagle's Liberty Belles Cheerleaders, in a straw vote, had named him one of the sexiest guys on the team. Ozzie was both single and boyishly handsome. He tried to keep a low profile, but it was never low enough for this fun-loving character to ever be comfortable under the judgmental scrutiny of his new coach. He even suffered a thinly veiled reference about being a heart throb in Stu Bykofsky's gossip column in The Philadelphia Daily News that fooled no one as to whom Stu was tagging. Ozzie hated that. Oh God, he hated that.

Ozzie's lease was up on his apartment in Blackwood, New Jersey, three weeks before training camp in July. His two roommates were also Eagles. They were California guys and wouldn't be back in town until the last minute, and Oz didn't want to sign a lease extension. Back in the 70s a ballplayer could get away with being out of town most of the off-season. As the only one available to sign a new lease, Ozzie feared if he didn't make the team, his roommates' antics might put him in a real estate jackpot while he was back in Texas waiting for the phone to ring. Ozzie was only four regular season games shy of qualifying for his NFL Players Association Lifetime Pension.

Ozzie knew about my storage room on the 200-level concourse. He asked me if we could stash his furniture there. If Oz made the team, he could always find an apartment. We moved his stuff in three trips.

Ozzie called me from training camp in West Chester as soon as he got the bad news. Told me "The Turk" sent him a message to come down to his office with his playbook, a one-way trip for the playbook. To a man, veteran players swore it was his best camp as an Eagle. Didn't matter, Oz was a goner.

Jerry Sisemore's wife was out of town with the kids. Size told Ozzie there was a key hidden under a flowerpot near the front door. I picked up Ozzie in West Chester and we spent the night in Sicklerville, New Jersey, drinking beer, shooting pool, and listening to The Rolling Stones singing "You can't always get what you want" until it was time to run Ozzie to the airport for a red eye back to San Antonio.

True to form, his flight attendants upgraded him to first class. As he headed down the ramp with one of them on his arm, I suddenly remembered his furniture. I yelled after him, "Yo Ozzie, what do you want me to do with your stuff?"

Over his shoulder came his exit line. "Put it on the fifty-yard line and burn it...I'm outta here."

I never thought about his stuff again until The Pope came to town.

The Papal visit, a historic, unprecedented event, was giving The City of Philadelphia fits planning for such an unprecedented crowd. Estimates exceeded a million-plus, but there was no realistic way of estimating how many of the faithful might show up. It's not like they were selling tickets, and this was shaping up to be the ultimate flash mob with rosary beads. The crowd coming into the city for the outdoor Papal Mass would be in addition to everyone coming into the city for work on a Wednesday. The only certainty: This could be the "Mother of all time" for crowd control, parking and traffic nightmares; a papal trifecta.

I wasn't the least concerned. It had nothing to do with me. I had the rare luxury of two consecutive nights off. The Spectrum and the Vet had no events scheduled, both would be dark. I was kicking back, heading down to the South Jersey shore for two days of Indian summer. Hallelujah! God bless the Pope. I'm outta here!

I almost made it to the bridge.

The voice was weirdly disembodied. It came out of the radio in my pickup truck. When it cut through the haze of me daydreaming of lying on the sand, I threw a ram, ran a red light and almost hit a man crossing the street. He was screaming at me. I was screaming at The Pope. I was screwed, palpably and Papally.

I'm thinking, "Sweet suffering shit, it's as if Stephen King, on acid, is writing the script of my life!"

The voice on the news channel confirmed details released only moments ago. "The City of Philadelphia has determined the best way to come into the City for those attending the Papal Mass on Logan Circle will be to use public transportation. Those who choose to drive are strongly urged to carpool and use the parking lots at The Philadelphia Sports Complex in Southeast Philadelphia, which will open at 4:30 a.m. Take the subway on the corner of Broad and Pattison to City Hall. Walk up the Parkway to Logan Circle."

It wasn't a bad idea for "the faithful," but for me it was Dante's Ninth Circle of Hell. I was in scramble city. I had no one available to work the largest parking event conceivable and less than two days to pull it off. I once had 120,000 Grateful Dead fans at JFK for three days in a row while the circus was in town at the Spectrum.

Elephant dung and acid heads, I may never get over that mixture, but it paled against my current Papal nightmare.

Every one of my supervisors had full-time day jobs, and all my cashiers and flag kids were in high school. None of them were available although at the very last minute the city mandated schools cancel all classes, but by then I had been forced to make some expedient, albeit frighteningly flaky, staffing decisions. I called in all my markers at Dobbs. I told Shamus, the doorman and bouncer, to round up the usual suspects. These were my friends: bar flies, bouncers, blue collar bon vivants and bartenders, most of whom I'd snuck into games at the Vet over the past few years. Betting on enough of them showing up was rolling the dice big time. I was dancing on the edge of extinction. Necessity is a mother hummer, but I'd trust Shamus with my life. Time and again, "Back to back, we denied the world access to our vulnerabilities."

I had one genuine over-riding concern. I couldn't rely on my ersatz crew to show up at 4:00 in the morning en masse and ready to work. These were night owls, but pre-dawn was well past their window of dependability. I put it on Shamus. He smiled at me, lifting a highball glass of Jamesons. "Why don't we have a sleepover at the Vet?"

I was still laughing when I realized he was serious, but knowing Shamus, I reasoned the positive results might outweigh the risks. Shamus was a good-time guy, but nobody fucked with him. If they did, they never did it twice.

The sleepover was on.

Deal was, we would rally at Dobbs at nine, I would buy burgers and pitchers of beer till eleven, then we'd caravan to the stadium. Once assembled I wasn't letting anybody in our net out of my sight. I had concerns specious of a party Mack and the boys threw for Doc in Steinbeck's Cannery Row. The boys got drunk, somebody threw a punch, furniture and friendships got broken and a thousand live frogs the boys captured for Doc's lab broke loose.

I told Shamus, "Nobody brings frogs" and to my surprise he got the allusion right away and started laughing. Nonetheless, I did not sleep well Monday night. I needn't have worried. As I said, nobody fucked with Shamus.

By midnight on Tuesday, my office was flooded with my ersatz emergency crew curled up in bedrolls and sleeping bags from wall to wall in my office on my AstroTurf covered floors. The storage area filled with Ozzie's furniture across the way on the far side of the concourse provided a double bed, daybed sofa, two overstuffed chairs and a giant beanbag which accommodated six more of us. In the dark, in the snoring dark, came a line I'll never forget. It was a moment of inspirational genius. I knew the voice. It was Mike McNally from The Electric Factory, a solid friend who had also done a stint bartending and managing the London Bar and Restaurant up in Fairmount.

"You know...if you just cleaned this place up and rearranged the stuff in here, this could be the coolest apartment in the world."

It was the "giddy up" for a great ride.

I always thought McNally was bright. I'd never thought of this. We all have our blind sides. Mike, I owe you.

October 2nd, 1979 was the first night I slept at the Vet. As the Pope-mobile rolled up Broad Street on its way from the airport to the alter, I stood with Joey Kohult on the ramp to the 400-level above Gate D watching a moment of history pass by. I'd never seen so many motorcycles.

Joey headed for the subway and I returned to rearranging Ozzie's stuff into the coolest apartment in the world. Early on, and I don't know why, we started referring to it as "The Secret Apartment." Almost like an "In your face, catch me if you can" dare. We never referred to the room by any other name.

A CHEESESTEAK FOR OZZIE

Ozzie, the former tight end with the Eagles, left town quickly with little more than the clothes on his back. He still had his pride and his dignity, but Philly was no place he wanted to be anymore. His red eye flight home came less than twelve hours after the Turk collected Ozzie's playbook and sent him on his way. It was over. Most of the team agreed Oz had a great camp and should have made the team. Team politics might have been involved, but the new coach with a bogus toupee that looked like it came out of a box of crackerjack made the decision. When a player is cut from the team all they want to do is be gone. Philly was in Ozzie's rear view mirror.

Oz had talent, real talent, and he had gas left in his tank. Some tight end somewhere would eventually go down in a crunch of bones, sinew and curses, and player personnel would be making calls. Ozzie sat by the phone. He needed to be on the roster of another team for only four more regular season games to be eligible for his NFL Players Association Pension when he reached fifty-five, but more than that he wanted to play football. Ozzie wasn't done with the dance.

His phone rang seven or eight games into the regular season. The Cardinals' backup tight end went down. Billy Bradley, "Number 28 in your program, number one in your heart" when he set team and NFL records as an Eagle, had retired in 1977 as a Cardinal. Billy had some juice with the Cards and told them Ozzie would be a good fit. They called Ozzie who flew up to Saint Louis for a tryout. They liked what they saw and signed him.

Oz called and told me the good news while sitting in his new apartment, a classy high rise near Saint Louis' famous archway to the West. Told me he could watch the local TV station's chopper fly through St. Louis' giant arch as he drank his morning coffee while listening to their report, seeing their helicopter on his TV as well as out his window. It was surreal. He'd landed on his feet. He was back in the game. Everybody I knew was happy for Ozzie.

His fourth game in a Cardinals' helmet would be in Philadelphia. How ironically perfect he'd earn his pension in the City of Brotherly Love at the Vet on November 18th. Our cowboy heart throb shared memories of nights in white satin with some of the most incredible women in Philadelphia, and he would return to get the magic number of games needed to give him his hard-earned pension.

The Cardinals came to town. They checked into their hotel near the stadium, and almost all of them did what teams do when they came to Philly. The team was heading uptown for a pre-curfew feast at Olde Original Bookbinders. A tourist trap, maybe, but a good one and these guys were tourists of sorts.

But not everyone wanted lobster tails. Ozzie called me to pick him up at his hotel. He knew the city and had a game plan of his own.

Oz wanted to go to Oregon Steaks just off Broad Street for a cheese steak, eaten standing up, watching old Italian men through the fence playing bocce ball on the other side of Oregon Avenue. When he came out of the hotel, he had a teammate with him. Ozzie knew what he missed and wanted in the Philly he loved; Bookbinders be damned.

As the Cardinals piled into cabs, Ozzie and his buddy jumped into the front seat of my pickup. Can't remember his friend's name, but remember the guy was a wide receiver known to be so fast he'd been tagged "Greased Lightning." Apparently, he earned the tag honestly.

Ozzie's description of what he guaranteed to be one of the best dining adventures in town had convinced his friend to forego Bookbinders. Lightning wanted a real Philly experience. Lobster he could get almost anywhere but a real Philly cheesesteak, one of the best in town according to his native guide, was something he might never get another shot at. No Bookbinders for Lightning. We headed to Oregon Avenue. Ozzie insisted it had to be his treat. When he placed his order, Oz spoke the words "Cheese wit" like a prayer.

Our stand-up dinner was awesome, flavored by a blistering argument in Italian by a gaggle of old paisans jabbering so graphically we didn't need an interpreter to follow their drift. It was so cold we couldn't tell their breath from cigar smoke as they played a game their ancestors enjoyed during the Roman Empire. Walking to the truck Lightning turned to us, smiling, saying, "To think I could have gone to Bookbinders."

Ozzie and Lightning had a team meeting before bed check, but there was a little time to play with. Oz told Lightning he wanted to make a quick stop at a place he knew in South Philly for a fast beer before I dropped them off at their hotel. I knew what he meant; Oz wanted to see the apartment before heading back. He'd never been there since we unloaded his stuff last August. He had never seen the room set up as a place to live.

Lightning did not know anything was up and just rolled with it as we neared the stadium. All the gates to the parking lots were padlocked, so I hopped a curb, driving down the sidewalk through a pedestrian gate. We circled the Vet and pulled up at my door, parked and went in. No reaction from Lightning who followed our lead, just looking around. We moved through my truck bay, passing the two small office rooms to the left, then through the double door opening into the inner ground level concourse. A little more looking around on Lightning's part, maybe a growing curiosity but still no reaction, no questions or comments. It made me think about the time McManus and I sprung this on Jay Haight not long ago.

I opened the door to The Secret Apartment. I turned on the lights. Over my shoulder Ozzie's teammate peered into the storeroom at the corridor of cardboard boxes, six-feet wide, stacked roughly seven-feet high on both sides. Not much to look at. Some of my toys, a kayak and a ten-speed bike rested on one side of the little "nothing to see here" hallway. "Lightning" paused beside the battered kayak, nodding approval. The corridor, almost forty feet long, seemed to go nowhere. Lightning, trusting Ozzie, his native guide, implicitly, still said nothing. We entered, he followed us into the box canyon.

He walked behind us with growing curiosity as we led Lightning to what looked to him to be a dead end.

We angled through the double blind and walked into the cavernous living area.

You could have heard Lightning's "Whoa!" from the subway stop on the corner of Broad and Pattison. Then he collapsed in a chair and started laughing.

Unlike Jay Haight, Lightning knew he had entered rare and uncharted territory.

Ozzie, always quick to take in the lay of the land, made himself at home, which in a way he certainly was. Opening the fridge, he grabbed a round of beers and passed them around. I put a record on the turntable. Mick Jagger reminded us one more time, "You can't always get what you want...." and the room filled up with stories, laughter and more than a few questions.

Oz approved of everything he saw, and Lightning loved the apartment and the ridiculous idea I lived in the Vet. He'd never been in our stadium before but had seen games played here on TV. He had endless questions, several times muttering something along the lines of "I can't believe this! I can't believe I'm inside the Vet the night before our game." He kept looking around and grinning like a little kid. Several times he jumped up and wandered around to inspect the room, loving the deceptive maze of boxes and the quixotic novelty of it all.

Lightning sat down, took a long pull on his beer and looked around, a great big smile on his face. He fully understood this was totally illegal and if I ever got caught there would be some serious repercussions. He was a little taken aback that something he knew had to be kept secret seemed to be so "in their face", particularly considering how easily we bopped into the stadium.

The pure insanity of living there the way I did was driving lightning crazy. He said it would be cool anywhere, but somehow, from all he knew of Philly sports, this was like living in the heart of the beast.

Ozzie indicated we had to watch the time as they had a brief team meeting before curfew. I started turning off lights and the artificial fireplace. Lightning looked wistful as he said, "You know, there was one thing... I know we couldn't do it, but it would have been great...." We looked at him. "It would have been incredible if we could have snuck out onto the field." He had never been out on the field of an opposing NFL team the night before a game.

I looked at Ozzie. He glanced at his watch and nodded.

We all stood up.

"Let's go."

We went out on the field. Lightning knew he was not in Kansas anymore. He was in the land of Oz. We walked around the field drinking our beers like we owned the place. There were no lights on anywhere. The moon played in and out of patches of clouds, while the stadium which surrounded us would roar tomorrow, but tonight sat ominously quiet.

Lightning put down his beer and crawled around on hands and knees, inspecting the playing surface. Lightning's biggest takeaway: How could anybody play on AstroTurf as terrible as ours? Even in the semi-darkness he kept finding seams and scary areas. I told him this was relatively new AstroTurf. He countered with "Your home field is the place where careers go to die." Ozzie and I couldn't disagree.

The guys made their team meeting with ten minutes to spare. I went home and roller skated the inner and outer loops of the 600-level beneath sometimes moonlight, sometimes dark. I think I achieved a state of childlike bliss.

The next day, November 18th, 1979, The Eagles beat The Cardinals 16 to 13 and Ozzie contributed with a crucial reception for a first down in the game that enabled him one day to receive his NFL Players' Association pension. Playing and training as much as he did on our AstroTurf, he damn well deserved it. It seemed fitting and just that Ozzie notched his pension game at The Vet.

A NIGHT TO REMEMBER

Here's something I touched on before, but this might never have occurred to many fans visiting the Vet. I will bet this would be true for tens of millions of fans who attended events in the Stadium. It's reasonable they might never have given this even a fleeting thought: The Vet was one of the gnarliest places for wild-ass edgy roller skating I have ever known. Think of her as a concrete Grand Canyon of challenges on wheels. Her ramps and circular loops were great places for mountain bike rides or long-distance runs, all with the promise you'll never see another living soul. The full rip was to be alone in the Vet beneath whatever light the night gave you, looping the 600-level, letting go of the cares that infest the day as you roll on silver wheels, falling in love again with unforgettable views of Philadelphia. Once you've seen the city this way you own it forever. You're as high above ground as you can be, rimming the outer edge of the big oval, maybe a hundred feet high, nothing but a thin rail between you and the city in the night. In my mind's eye, I can still see her from what was, at that time, the highest view available. There you are, on roller skates, so comfortable you forgot they aren't part of you, alive with the night, reveling in one of greatest views of The City of Brotherly Love that ever existed.

I've never felt so childlike—free.

In a word, it was bliss.

The Vet became my sacred plaything. I loved her as I would one day love the woman of my dreams. I couldn't get enough of her. I never thought of this when I lived in the stadium but my relationship with her was schizophrenic in that I often shared the stadium with over sixty-five thousand others at raucous sporting events in the evening only to sit hours later, high in the stadium, alone in a profound silence when everyone had gone home. In a way, I hadn't left but had gone home too. Sitting in the top row of the 700-level, meditating at times like this, drove me inside myself to where my deepest meanings were. Such times could be life altering if you let them in. I needed to let them in.

If you knew the stadium well and had the incredible opportunity to spend enough time alone with her, you came to grips with something just beyond the feathered edge of reality. Some residue of life and fantasy was there, some spirit and energy from the fans seeped into the steel and concrete. Something ineffable took on a life of its own and lived there. The Vet could be unoccupied, but she was never empty. In her essence lived so many incredibly vivid and wonderful Philadelphian sports memories. Memories of joy and heartbreak mingled over the years. At night, when the Vet was dark and empty, its spirit to me was a palliative.

One singular night stands by itself from my time there. Sometime in football season, maybe late October, in the middle of the week, I'd jumped into a cab coming back from J. C. Dobbs bar on South Street as a storm rolled in. It had to be late, definitely after midnight. The driver laughed when I asked him to drop me off at the stadium.

Cabby let me out on the corner of Broad and Pattison by the subway stop. He didn't drive away at first, watching me as I stood in front of Connie Mack's Statue fumbling for my keys in flashes of lightning before ambling over to my door beneath Gate D. I made cover as it started to rain. I thought I'd work out some of my demons on a midnight terror-tour of the Stadium before turning in. Sometimes I'd ride my 10- speed bike but on this night, I went out on roller skates. I had the greatest pair of roller skates. The skates didn't belong to me, but they were mine to use for the season, meaning the football season. The skates were California beauties, custom made in LA, state of the art. They belonged to Terry Tautolo, number 58, a linebacker who had played for Vermeil at UCLA the year they won The Rose Bowl. Terry was contractually forbidden, as were all his teammates, from physical activities that could injure or incapacitate him during the season. Since he couldn't use them and we had the same shoe size, Terry let me have them for the season.

Terry's home was in Long Beach, California, and those kids knew skates. These weren't roller blades but professional grade high top leather skates with reworked custom wheels. Every advantage factored in for maximum control and performance. I used to rip up the Vet at night. No one was ever around, excepting one or two guys in the security office next to the Phillies Offices near Gate B. When the Vet was dark it was "no man's land."

I went into the apartment, not ready for bed, and rolled out for a hell-raising blast on the ramps. I circled the 200- level concourse, under cover because it seemed to be raining harder, taking a ramp to the 300-level which is also undercover but offers great views of the field looking down from atop the 300-level seats. The Vet in moonlight is an endorphin rush but this night offered something else, an eerily dark night pierced by violent flashes of lightning, the view of the field and city coming in spectacular intermittent strobes. I ramped up to the 600- level. If I had to choose a favorite level for skating or bike riding in the Stadium, it would have to be the 600-level concourse with those incredible views of the city while protected from weather under the slope of the 700-level seats above. If it wasn't raining or snowing, the walkways circling the field between the 200 and 300-level seats and the walkway upstairs between the 500 and 600-level seats both offered great views of the field also.

One other great loop, but only if it wasn't raining: I loved taking my bike or skates up to the 12-foot-wide walkway at the very top of the 700-level seats. After the Phils won the World Series in 1980, aluminum bleachers were installed on the walkway creating thousands of additional seats. That killed riding around the top of the Vet but, before that happened, when it was still possible, it was awesome.

On this October night I worked my way up to the 600-level concourse and racked up several loops. The view in the thunder and lightning storm was addictive. A loop was roughly somewhere around a half mile, and I must have racked up several miles before I headed back down the ramps. There were only two elevators in the Stadium back then, both inside the stadium, one by Gate H and one near Gate B, next to The Phillies office. Both elevators only went up to the 400-level, which housed the press box and what passed for luxury boxes at the time. The 400 was home to The Eagles, City Offices and Press Boxes as well as The Stadium Club Bar and Restaurant. The Stadium Club was open to the public, but you still needed a ticket to get into the stadium. Only the elevator by Gate H went underground to the 100-level where locker rooms, Nilon Brothers and City maintenance areas were located.

I'm flying down the ramps that night, pushing the edge, skidding turns. I'm getting ready to turn in but decided on one last run all the way underground to the 100-level thinking I'd ride the elevator back up to the 400-level near The Stadium Club, then run ramps back down to the 200 before looping around to the secret apartment to call it a night. I was feeling my oats and running the ramps with abandon, having a ball.

I'm on the fly, in skate park heaven. I'm coming down the ramps at breakneck speed skidding turns. At the bottom of the 100-level ramp, I'm approaching the elevator on the edge of control. Suddenly the elevator doors started to open.

I wasn't alone.

I'd been thrown off my game when the elevator doors began to open. In the second I realized something was amiss, I flew into the elevator much too fast to be in control. My feet went out from under me. I saw someone, hearing a scream as I hit the rear wall. A man crouched protectively in the corner. We were both making startled noises. Nothing was cool. Silver round film canisters flew everywhere, clattering to the floor. The man had been holding a stack of them when I invaded his space like some banshee on wheels. He took one corner, I the other. Startled, he looked at me with giant cow eyes, his mouth forming a large gaping "O". He probably saw the same expression on my face. Neither of us spoke. What would you say? I should have muttered some apology but was stunned into silence. It was rude of me. The word "gob smacked" comes to mind, too much overload to take in.

Before either of us could speak, the doors closed, and the elevator started to rise, heading back up to the fourth floor. We avoided eye contact, staring awkwardly straight ahead.

I knew who he was. I doubt if he knew me.

I had often heard Dick Vermeil sometimes worked all night before big games, watching films and catching some sleep on a couch in his office. This had to be one of those nights. I never knew what Coach was doing in the elevator that night. We never talked about it. I suspect he was taking a stack of game films down to the locker room to exchange them for some others or something like that, as he was holding a tall stack of them when I invaded his space in the elevator, going down in my groaning crash. In the awkward silence after our combined startled screams I had clawed at the rail, pulling myself to my feet, dazed, everything hurting. As the elevator rose slowly, we looked warily at each other. I didn't know what to say. I know I should have apologized. I was embarrassed. The elevator came to a stop. The doors opened. We nodded to each other, still saying nothing. I skated into the night.

Being around the building all the time, it was inevitable that we'd occasionally run into each other, but we never had occasion to speak about our nutso midnight run in. I was never in his company where it could come up.

I don't even know if he'd be able to pick me out of a lineup and I had the advantage on that count in recognizing him since he was famous, everybody knew him. I was never sure after this incident if I was ever anywhere in his proximity where he might see me, if Coach Vermeil was looking at me wondering if I was, or was not, *that* guy from *that* night. The experience confirmed for me the notion that in traumatic situations, eyewitness identifications aren't always reliable.

I'll probably never know what went through his mind that night or how he remembered it. I'm sorry I put him out in any way and wished I'd apologized. I was wrong to invade his space as I did, and didn't see it coming, nor know what to say at the time. Half of this story belongs to him and I hope he got to tell it sometime in good spirits.

TWO FAVORITE MEMORIES

The 1980 World Series and the 1981 NFC Title game produced two of my favorite sports memories in the stadium. Both occurred within three months of each other. The first was Pete Rose's barehanded save of a foul ball fly in front of the Phillies' dugout when the ball popped out of Bob Boone's catcher's mitt. It was one of those iconic moments burned into my love of the game. It gave us the 2nd out in the last inning of game six. We could taste the win. Mounted policemen ringed the field; Tugger on the mound. Rose, one of those ballplayers with an intensely gifted game sense, was exactly where he had to be in a cosmic moment. No one who saw this happen, whether in the stands or on TV, will ever forget his timely save, nor Pete's gesture when he jogged towards Tug and flipped him the ball. Rose held one forefinger up. One more out and the crown's ours. Sweet....

.... but there is something else of import in this scene that not everyone watching might have noticed. When Tug caught the ball tossed to him by Pete Rose, he glanced over at Mike Schmidt on third. Something whimsical occurred in that moment, and it might have changed everything.

John McManus, Tug's closest friend, always said McGraw had more Zen in him than Tug realized. McManus was sort of right. With Tug, it was not always about what it was about. In this brief spasm of time, horseshit may have played a small but significant part in helping Tug win The World Series.

The Philadelphia Police Department had no illusions about what winning the pennant could unleash. To control the crowd which might storm the field, the authorities lined the field with mounted policemen. A string of horses protected the field behind Schmidt. McGraw facing phenomenal mind-numbing pressure looked past Schmidt, dwarfed by almost 1500 pounds of horse and rider. Tug grinned, amused by whatever whimsical humor he found in the moment as the horse behind Schmidt unleashed a world-class steaming dump that even made several police dogs nearby scurry away in disgust. The image took Tug out of the moment. Of all the things he might be, or should be, contemplating, maybe some of McManus' insight to that fluttering streak of Zen in Tug came into play. A pressure releasing whimsical moment could well have eased Tug into fifth gear, allowing him to fan Willie Wilson and win the Series and a Baby Ruth. Willie never had a chance.

The boys who shared milkshakes in a red Corvette convertible on their way to work that day were about to drink champagne and celebrate as if they had just sacked the city which in a way they had. I'll clarify the milkshake allusion down the road a bit, but not here.

The Phillies won the first World Series in franchise history.

Schmidt was honored as our most valuable player.

Tug took home another MVP, the coveted Babe Ruth Award.

Then the boys of summer popped some corks.

My second favorite sports moment came three months later, on a frigid January afternoon when the Eagles running back, Wilbert Montgomery, slid into the secondary on a 42-yard touchdown run that broke the Cowboys' backs, the momentum of the game never again an issue. Wilbert slipped through the right side of the line in a hole created by offensive tackle Jerry Sisemore, who mugged "Two Tall" Jones. Jerry owned Jones. Nobody laid a finger on Wilbert. Jones did not even pursue him. Sisemore manhandled Jones so far out of the play it was pointless for "Too Tall" to even go after Wilbert. Jones just stood there, "faced." Every move Jones made during that iconic play had been off balance as he stumbled backwards. For Jones, the play was over when the center snapped the ball. He was history before Wilbert touched the ball. The reason I love this play was Sisemore's quiet control. Jerry's an unassuming guy, humble to a fault. He "came up" in '73, first-round draft pick, started his first game, holding that honor for over ten years. Most fans never fully grasp what an incredible feat it is to step into the starting lineup on the offensive line as a rookie. Jerry not only did this, but over the years notched a few Pro Bowls on his belt. Somebody in player personnel really knew what they were doing when they offered Jerry a contract. He made that touchdown happen, but the spotlight rarely shines on men in the trenches unless they're called for holding or missing an assigned block and gotten their quarterback crushed.

But I must make a confession here. I did not see Jerry's block or the end of Wilbert's run in real-time, even though I was there on the walkway between the 500 and 600-level seats. I had been out on the 600-level concourse on my walkie-talkie confirming something with security out in the lots. I had just come in from the outer concourse to circle the field on the walkway between the 500 and 600- level seats. I did see the start of the run, just another play from scrimmage but when Wilbert came through the line, it was obvious that no Cowboy would be able to lay a hand on him. I turned my back on the game and looked up at the fans in the 600 and 700-level seats, every one of them on their feet, screaming in long-awaited joy as the Birds crushed the Cowboys on our home turf. I knew I would see this play countless times on film, but the rapture of all those Eagles fans would be something that belonged to the moment alone, so I stopped to watch them. I'm not sorry I did.

Those fans and my living memory of them are symbolic of the intense spirit I was reaching for to honor in the dedication of this book. That day they would have bleed green. The day belonged to them; the team happy to give it to them. The quintessential football experience so overwhelming, the stadium becomes a church where heathens come to pray. It has to take place in a building without a roof, open to the sky. Their fervor would have blown the lid off.

I encourage anyone reading this to check out this play on "You Tube" from the NFC championship game and focus on Jerry Sisemore's complete dominance of "Too Tall" Jones. Spoil yourself, watch Wilbert a few times, but then watch again and focus on what you might not have seen before. Look at the man in the trenches, number 76, who made it happen.

It was a clinic.

Sisemore took Jones to school.

McMANUS AND McGRAW

Johnny McManus and Tug McGraw met at The London after Tug moved to Perot Street, in the late 80s or early 90s. John tended bar doubling as madman in residence. A straight odd couple, they naturally became best buds raising some good fun and holy hell together. Tug loved to hear John tell him about the Secret Apartment, which he had no knowledge of when he spent time at the Vet "in the show."

Those two talked about writing a book together about the year The Phillies beat The Royals to win The World Series. Title would be *From Milkshakes to Champagne* from the notion that Tug, and Mike Schmidt lived near each other in the Media zip code. They'd often drive into the ballpark together, usually in Schmidt's top down shiny red Corvette.

The night they won The World Series, McGraw and Schmidt stopped for milkshakes at Five Points in Media on their way to the game. You know how that night ended.

McManus and McGraw never wrote the book.

McManus and McGraw both died in 2004, eleven months apart.

The Vet went down that year also.

I watched it implode on the evening news and thought of the

stray cats that lived there. I like cats; they seem to live with us on their own terms. The ones I knew at the Vet from my time there certainly did, and I hoped most of them moved out when nobody was around anymore. I knew none of them could survive the implosion. No cat could ever run that fast.

HAULING TUG'S ASHES

Tug passed away on January 5th, 2004 at his son Tim's spread out in Tennessee. John McManus was there with Tug's older brother, Hank, and they brought some of Tugger's ashes back to Philadelphia. John told me Tug was holding a baseball in his left hand to his last full breath.

McManus related this story to me at the far end of The Lucky Seven Bar on Aspen up in Fairmount. Jud Bertholf, the owner, was behind the bar serving drinks and heard some of this story also.

Hank contacted Bill Giles at The Phillies and received permission to place some of Tug's ashes in the pitcher's mound at the Vet. It seemed fitting, and just that something of him would rest on the spot where he had helped bring us a World Championship. Hank and McManus went down to the stadium and sprinkled some of Tug's ashes on the mound sometime before the Vet imploded on March 21st, 2004.

When McManus told me this, I mentioned a recent article I'd seen in The Daily News claiming The Phillies had transferred some of the old mound to the new stadium in a gesture of continuity from their past to the future. John hadn't heard this, and I asked him if he thought they would've known to scoop up all of Tug's ashes or maybe left some of them to be buried beneath what would become the parking lot on the corner of Broad and Pattison near the subway stop. John thought for second, shook his head very slowly, and said he could not know. "I can't answer questions such as yours" he said laughing at a line he loved from Zorba the Greek.

We were drinking shots of Jameson.

I said, "So you're telling me you actually don't know where Tug's ashes really are? You guys lost Tug's ashes."

McManus got this funny look on his face. Johnny had this weird cackling laugh when something he found funny drilled down inside him. He could barely get the words out: "Tug'd be down with that. He never knew where the hell he was half the time anyway."

I recently learned while researching information for these Vet stories that during the 2008 World Series Tug's son Tim was invited to throw out the first pitch of game 3 in the new Phillies ballpark. At that time, he sprinkled some of Tug's ashes on the pitcher's mound. So, we know for certain something of Tug is still with us. We'll never know if some of the ashes from Hank McGraw and John McManus' earlier effort made it over to the new park, but from what I knew of Tug I have to believe that one way or another he would've found a way to be there when we needed him. Phillies won games 3, 4 and 5 at home to take the 2008 World Series 4 to 1 against Tampa Bay.

In more than spirit, Tug was on the mound.

McManus died days before Christmas from complications of pneumonia and a lifetime of chain-smoking Marlboros and a Tom Waits late night lifestyle.

2004 was a rough year: Tug, the Vet, and McManus. Damn.

INSTANT REPLAY

The scene is a bar in heaven
Two Irishmen, McManus and McGraw
Guys born to sit on bar stools telling stories,
Hunch over mason jars of Jameson and foamy dark Guinness
Stunningly exotic women flirt with them.
There is no tab, all drinks are on the house.
There is no last call, McManus can even smoke again.
Hey, it is heaven!
On a giant flatscreen TV mounted on the wall
The two men watch various scenes from their lives.
An edited collage, all the good stuff.
McManus wants the remote
McGraw won't give it up.
Most of the time they laugh,
but sometimes they look away,
A wisp of smoke in their eyes,
Or maybe they miss us, the way we miss them.
Tug turns to John.
Draws down a heroic mouthful of Guinness,

Nods towards activities on the screen:

The final cut, the rerun of their lives.

Tug wonders aloud,

"What the hell was *that* all about?"

They laugh incoherently,

Something funny to them beyond comprehension, McManus mumbling

"...Had to be there, Frank, had to be there...."

He wistfully blows a thin blue stream of smoke at the screen,

McManus becomes strangely apprehensive,

Asking, "Can we come here again, Frank?"

McGraw sips his Jameson.

To Tug it's a religious experience.

He answers softly

"Every night, m'boyo, every night...."

Instant Replay was submitted in my absence to be read at John McManus' Celebration of Life: Rembrandts, 20 January 2005. Our daughter Tara was married on a beach in Playa del Carmen, Mexico, that day. I had committed to be one of the speakers at John's tribute but when I was told the event would be on the 20th, I couldn't make it due to long-established plans for Tara's wedding so I wrote and submitted Instant Replay for the event. Tara and her husband Curt own Urban Jungle on Passyunk Avenue near the corner of 11th and Tasker in South Philly. Check out their Jungle sometime.

Alive in our hearts, taken from us in 2004

John McManus, Frank McGraw, and Veterans Stadium

"To Live in the hearts

Of those we leave behind

Is not to die."

From a plaque on the wall of The Naval-Marine Memorial Stadium in Annapolis, Maryland, dedicated to members of The Class of 1951 killed in The Korean War

IS THAT WHO I THINK IT IS?

The most well-known and unlikely person I ever snuck into any event at Veteran's Stadium was an incredibly gifted and well-known athlete. He was also a humble man and had he gone up to any gate and explained his situation, he would easily have gained admission, as most likely he was going to be a guest for the game in either The Mayor's or Leonard Tose's Box. All he needed to do was get into the building and take the elevator to the fourth level. He certainly did not need me at all, as no usher at any gate would have turned him away.

The occasion, a one p.m. Eagles Game, late November. The weather unseasonably pleasant for the time of year. I was on the sidewalk just inside the main gate to the north parking lot from Pattison Avenue. I had a walkie-talkie, monitoring reports from all the north lot gates on Broad, Packer and 10th Street as to when I had to close our largest lot and shift traffic flow to the lots south of Pattison. It's a critical move, but I'd been doing it for several years and everything was copasetic. We'd easily park 12,000 cars this day, no sweat.

I spotted him coming at least fifty yards away in a crowd, crossing Pattison Avenue at the corner of 11th Street. The light had just changed. What struck me most was not who he was but that in the cluster of fifty fans heading to the game, no one seemed to realize he was among them. Recognizing him, I knew he would have parked in the S4 VIP lot near the statue of Kate Smith on the sidewalk by the entrance to the Ovations Club on the opposite side of the Spectrum, the only lot Sixers or Flyers ever used. In the cluster crossing Pattison from the south lots, I had spotted him right away. He towered over everyone else and as a beloved and admired Philadelphian sports icon had one of the most recognizable faces in town. But in that crowd hustling to get into the Vet he was just another anonymous fan, a father protectively shepherding two small boys across a busy street. I watched him break away from a growing crowd heading up the ramps by gate H to stay on Street level and head under the overhang of the 300-level walkway circling the Stadium. He veered right, away from the door to the 4th floor elevator, and over to the oversized eight-foot-tall door of The Sixers front offices, probably thinking he'd get into the Vet that way. If somebody was supposed to meet him, they didn't get the memo.

The man was Julius Erving, "Doctor J", the Philadelphia Seventy-Sixer's internationally known superstar. He was one of the reasons the Sixers had such a dramatically high door. The door was locked. Doc rattled the door, knocked several times and turned, saying something to the boys, his sons. I was halfway over there by then.

I gave the order to close the north lots before I got to him. I told all stations I would be going silent for a short time, but call me if anything went nuclear. I had a good crew, and they always had my back. I approached our six-million-dollar man.

"Hi Doctor J. Sir, do you need to get into the building? I've got a key" He looked at me a bit exasperated, noted that I had a walkie-talkie radio in one hand and a key in the other and realized he'd been saved.

Doc told me he was trying to get into the Stadium. He and his boys were going to the game as guests in Leonard Tose's private box. He knew where to go once he got inside. Someone was supposed to let him in through the Sixers door, but there was a screwup.

"No sweat, Doc, we got this covered, follow me." We took off.

By the time we got to my office door, Dr. J's kids seemed more relaxed. That didn't last long as a group of about ten of my friends stood outside my door waiting for me. One of them was a friend, a lawyer from Media. His nickname was "Shoey." It may have been a play on a character from Star Wars, but I can't remember why. Shoey's hard to describe but "fun loving, delightful and harmless" are good starting points. I won't even try to explain Shoey. Best I can do here is describe what alarmed Dr. J's boys making them cling to their father for protection. Shoey was in "game mode," dressed for the occasion. He sported a green head covering that looked like an oversized beret much like you might see on a Bellini Portrait of a Doge of Venice. His skin was green, his dangling earrings were green. Shoey wore a green cape over a green tunic and had ruffled green pantaloons over green tights, all topped off with green pointy shoes with curled toes. Dr. J did a stutter step when he saw Shoey, maybe caught unawares in a "what the hell have I gotten us into" moment. One of Doctor J's boys gave out a muffled, frightened moan.

"I've got this," I said, stepping in front of them, producing my magic key to the kingdom. We all went through the door, my friends knowing the drill, parted, allowing The Irvings to pass through the scrum, the boys tucked beneath their father's protective wings like little birds. The odd assembly, Shoey now in the lead, crossed my equipment bay area to a double door at the back to the inner 200-level concourse, which I unlocked. I explained to Doctor J where we were and how to get to the elevator up to the Eagles offices on the 400-level and Tose's private box.

Dr. J turned, shook my hand and thanked me. He didn't need me to get in but wasn't the kind of guy comfortable bulling his way past a guard when his connection got screwed up. He appreciated a "native guide." As they walked away, both of his sons never took their eyes off Shoey as the wild man in the green cape disappeared into the crowd.

THERE IS NO DIRECTOR OF PARKING

I can't remember the hot button issue that started this rolling, but one night just before an event at the Spectrum something happened, and I needed to find Joe Yank to solve a problem at warp speed. I ran up to an entrance and tried to get into the building. The guards were not having any of it, and precious time was lost. In their defense, anybody working a gate at a Philadelphia sports event has heard it all, over time, and gullible they are not.

Joe Yank was head of event security at the Spectrum. Everybody knew and loved Joe Yank. Joe had been with Patton in World War II and had a no-nonsense way of getting things done. His real name was Joe Iancale and nobody in the Army ever pronounced his name correctly, so he had picked up the nickname "Joe Yank." He wore the name proudly all his life. Joe even had a "Y" in the center of his front door, and I know some of the people Joe dealt with never knew his last name wasn't really "Yank."

Whatever brought us together that night got somehow resolved and afterwards Joe suggested I check in with Steve Flynn's secretary, Lorraine, and get an official Spectrum photo ID so I could get to him faster in emergencies. Flynn was a former FBI guy and Joe's boss. A Spectrum ID was a good idea. I told Joe I would take him up on it.

I'd never had an ID for the Vet, an oversight that hadn't come up, strangely enough, so I requested one from Nilon Brothers. Someone in their office told me a part-time administrative assistant who was a high school student from Maria Goretti Catholic could hook me up when she came in later that day. I can't remember her name, but she was a good kid, I think she was a 10th grader, and I'd seen her around the office.

The Goretti girl took a Polaroid photo of me and asked a few questions as she sat at her typewriter creating the card. She came to the line for a job description and paused, asking what I did. I thought a moment and said, "Director of Parking Operations, Philadelphia Sports Complex."

Maria Goretti didn't give it a second thought, typed what I told her in the appropriate blank, then sealed the photo ID in plastic. My official Veteran's Stadium photo ID had been pre-signed by Joel Ralph, the Commissioner of Parks and Recreation, head man for the City at the Sports Complex.

Called Steve Flynn, who okayed an ID and told me to get in touch with Lorraine. She would get me a Spectrum ID.

Jumped in my golf cart and headed over to the Spectrum. I was now sitting in Lorraine's office. She had taken my photo and was preparing a Spectrum form similar to the one Maria Goretti's finest had given me at the Vet. Everything went along smoothly until Lorraine asked for my job title. I told her I was "The Director of Parking Operations for The Philadelphia Sports Complex."

Lorraine stopped typing.

She smiled and looked up at me.

Lorraine was a senior administrative assistant at the Spectrum. Lorraine moved in the fast lane; a major leaguer involved in several hundred sold-out events yearly. She'd been doing this for several years, was good at her job and knew the ropes. Lorraine was no 10th grade high school student who worked part time after school three days a week. Lorraine was amused but definitely not buying it.

"There is no Director of Parking Operations" she said, shaking her head but laughing pleasantly.

I slid my Vet Stadium photo ID across her desk. She looked at it, looked at me, smiled again and with an endearing whimsical giggle, typed "Director of Parking Operations" in the appropriate space.

Those IDs were like Willie Wonka's golden tickets, though I never really needed my ID at the Vet as I had my own door. The Spectrum ID however was a much different story. I now had a season ticket to all Sixers, Flyers and every other event at literally some of the greatest shows on earth.

But Lorraine was right. There never was a Director of Parking for the Sports Complex. I simply ran the parking lots.

OTHO NEVER KNEW

Otho Davis wore black. In his black Levi's and black Nocona Cowboy boots, this Texan transplant shuffled around the Vet like the stadium's version of Johnny Cash. Otho, head trainer for the Philadelphia Eagles during my time in the stadium, was a good old boy from Elgin, Texas, a town famous for making bricks and the pejorative expression "Dumber than an Elgin Brick." Otho might have been from Elgin but he was anything but stupid. He knew more about things going on behind the scenes at the stadium than most people, but he never knew about my living there. That's funny to me because Otho was the only person I knew of who enabled others to live there.

Had Otho ever gotten wind of my living in the stadium, I would've been in trouble. I considered Otho a major security threat to my secret. Otho might mention my apartment to Rusty Sweeney, the Eagles's equipment manager. And Rusty would almost certainly have told one of his closest friends, who happened to work for Nilon Brothers, and he sure as hell would have told my Uncle Jack. There were networks of people in the stadium you had to be aware of.

Every football season Otho took under his wing a college intern majoring in sports medicine to work for and be trained by Otho for credit towards a physical therapy degree. Working under

Otho and his assistant, Ron O'Neal was an incredible "hands-on" experience. Ron O' left the Eagles in the early eighties to take on the Head Trainer position for The Patriots and was highly respected by the team.

Ron O' was deeply missed when he left town.

Otho sweetened the deal he had with the college interns by offering them a free place to stay during their semester in Philly. It was a singularly unique, once in a lifetime opportunity because they would be hunkering down in the Vet. Living in the locker room, how cool is that?

They did not actually live "in the locker room" but "under the locker room" or more accurately under the slope of the 200-level seats. Their sleeping area was crude and almost down at field level in an area only few people ever knew about, and even fewer had ever seen. It is charitable, as well as a stretch of the imagination, to call their sleeping area even a crawl space. The entrance to their sleeping area was through a door in Rusty Sweeney's equipment room. Their cot was at the bottom of a long, roughly 25-degree slope of poured concrete that resembled a hardened whitish lava flow. It was so primitive I'm sure the interns only slept there, having free run of the locker rooms that offered them carpeted floors, a TV, comfortable seating, refrigerator, some version of a cooking area, showers, washroom, weight room and hot tub. Not for everyone but in the world of sports; a veritable "man cave heaven."

I only ever ran into one of these guys when he was heading towards the stadium crossing the parking lot with two large grocery bags. I had seen him a few times in the locker room and gave him a ride into the building in my modified golf cart. I can't remember his name, but he was a likeable guy, an Asian-American who interned circa 1980. As I never ran into any of Otho`s interns at any other time in the stadium, I am certain one of his ground rules was that his interns maintain an extremely low profile.

Otho's interns had 24/7 access to the stadium through a door on street level beneath Gate H which was also the door closest to the elevator. One flight down to the 100-level underground where the training room and locker rooms were located was where I'd crashed into Vermeil that night in my roller-skating fiasco. The elevator also went up to the fourth level, no stops in between, to the City and Eagles Offices and the Stadium Club Bar and Restaurant. The entrance allowed Otho's interns access to the building without having to go through the security entrance on ground level under Gate B. I doubt security ever knew the interns were even in the building but do not know this for certain.

I know from my own time in the stadium the interns' experience had to be a benchmark time in their lives. I think they have a link on Facebook and keep in touch. I imagine there are a few dozen guys who spent a season there with stories of the time they spent in the Vet. I know it was a tradition that they all signed the wall down where they slept. Their signatures buried now deep beneath the parking lot on the corner of Broad and Pattison, the memory alive in a place where only they can go.

But all this only serves to set up a story involving the Eagles head trainer, Otho Davis, and the All Pro lineman, Jerry Sisemore in the off season in 1980 or 1981. It would have been early in the year and Otho wanted Jerry to fly up from his home at The Rock Marina on Lake Travis near Austin, Texas, to see "Doctor D." Dr. DiStefano was the team's sports medicine surgeon operating out of Paoli General. Jerry had been nursing an injury which would have sidelined a weaker man but never stopped him from playing hurt and playing way above the cut. The issue seemed to be, would it be better to stay with the ongoing intensive therapy and play through pain or was the situation serious enough for some minor surgery, which if done immediately could allow him to be fully healed before summer camp in July. Otho planned everything for the trip north.

"Size" would fly to Philly, take a cab to the hotel at 10th and Packer across from the north east corner of the north lot and check in with Otho the following morning. Otho would send a car to pick him up and bring Jerry to the training room in the Vet for a "catchup" before running him out to Paoli to see Doctor D.

Jerry had other plans. I picked him up at the airport and we headed for the crap tables in Atlantic City. It wasn't going to be a late night and before midnight we ended up in left field high enough in the 300-level seats to be under cover as rolling thunder and flashes of lightning strobe lit the field in dramatic streaks of light. We sat topping off our night with an ice bucket of "long necks" while consuming dripping "cheese wits" from Geno's Steaks. The field before us was set up for the start of the upcoming baseball season weeks away. A mist rolled across the field. If you ever loved the Vet, this was heaven. It was late March but not so cold we felt uncomfortable, the moment too dramatically charged to be aware of the weather. We turned in as it started to rain.

There was both a double bed and a daybed in the Secret Apartment. Jerry nodded off on the daybed to the sounds of thunder and lightning. The apartment was like being in a bunker.

I awoke to the smell of coffee and the sound of Tom T. Hall singing "Faster Horses" on the stereo. Jerry grew up in the Texas Panhandle. He has the soul of a ranch hand and is always up before the sun. However, there was not any sun in the forecast this day and Jerry had his first cup of coffee sitting outside at the top of the 300-level seats, undercover, out of the rain. Jerry told me he'd been reflecting on the incredible benefits a kid from the panhandle had come to enjoy from his time down on that playing field. He didn't take anything for granted and appreciated deeply how his long, strange journey had brought him to a place he'd always love. For

Jerry Sisemore to sit quietly in the empty stadium, alone with his memories and the awe he felt for the Vet, was for him, a deeply spiritual experience.

Jerry handed me a cup of coffee and gave me a weather report.

"Tommy...it's like a monsoon out there." We hung out a while, had another round of coffee with some pastry I laid in from Termini Brothers on 8th. Jerry looked at his watch. "Better check in with Otho." He used the wall phone. Jerry got Otho on the horn in the Eagles' training room downstairs and they talked briefly. From what I could hear, Jerry was reassuring a somewhat panicked Otho who had been calling the hotel only to find out Jerry had never checked in. Otho knowing it was raining hard wanted to send a car to bring him to the stadium. Jerry thanked Otho, said he would see him in 10 minutes, didn't need a ride, and hung up.

Minutes later Jerry headed out the door with his coat over his shoulder, a cup of coffee in one hand, his overnight bag in the other.

As Jerry walked into the locker room, Otho came up to him, smiling in relief. Two teammates came in right after Jerry and they all stood around together catching up. Up till then the euphoria of old friends reuniting had carried the moment. Suddenly something struck Otho and his expression turned to bemusement. The two guys who had come in after Jerry were soaking wet. Jerry was bone dry. Otho wanted to know how Jerry got there without getting wet and Jerry would not tell him saying it would be his little secret. He did muddy the waters by allowing he had not gotten a ride and had walked. Jerry knew something like this would drive Otho nuts. Otho knew Jerry, knew he wouldn't lie. Jerry was honest to a fault. The situation was loaded, a guy thing, distilled to the pure essence of old friends busting balls.

Over the next few years while the two men were still with The Eagles, Otho must have pursued this mystery easily a hundred times. Otho needed to know everything. It was his nature. He never let it rest. Even during games, when the defense was on the field, Otho would walk along side of Jerry asking if he was ever going to tell him about that rainy morning. If you wanted to talk to Sisemore when the offense wasn't on the field, you had to walk with him because his intensity was such that he never stood still when not in play. He paced back and forth behind the player's bench, pacing like a caged grizzly bear. A locker room joke said Jerry would someday be charged with the cost of replacing the strip of AstroTurf he wore out with his relentless pacing. His intensity made Sisemore the blue-chip player he was.

"You're never gonna tell me, are you, Jerry?"

"Nope. Otho, this one you're never gonna figure out. It's my secret."

Jerry never gave it up.

Otho never knew.

He hated not knowing.

Otho never figured it out.

We loved it because we knew it drove Otho nuts.

LIGHTS! GET IT? LIGHTS!

The Phillies had taken the first two games of the 1980 World Series at home at the Vet to lead The Kansas City Royals two to zip. When game two was still underway and my duties in the lots wrapped up, I'd joined an obscene amount of friends I'd snuck into the game at the top of the 300-level seats looking down on 1st base, for what turned out to be a nail biter. The Phillies pulled it out in the eighth with four come from behind runs to send The Royals packing with a six to four loss. The next three games would be on the road in Kansas City. The mood in Philadelphia was upbeat and euphoric. Philadelphians, starved for a pennant, could taste victory. You would have thought we'd already won the Series.

I heard ABC booked The Stadium Club for an after-game party and headed up to the fourth level to celebrate. I dragged an old friend, Joey Kohult, with me and we blew past security and headed to the bar for a couple of beers. The bar located on the lowest tier of the terraced club, easily a hundred feet long, offered a view of the field from above first base through an unobstructed glass wall. To stand there with a cold beer in hand, two up in the World Series surrounded by remarkable women looking down on the field where you'd just witnessed a crushing come-from-behind victory has to be a sport's fans notion of heaven. The room was filled with network bigwigs, celebrities, sponsors and their guests. Joey and I didn't belong there, but it was too good to pass up. We mingled.

A tour of the terraced levels of the club brought us to an interesting spot to be a pair of flies on the wall. Joey and I spotted him at the same time and without a word sidled up to the edge of a group of about six partygoers; five of them drop dead beautiful high-maintenance women and one bombastic high-profile megalomaniac elderly man. He was telling a long-winded story. The women were fawning all over him and hanging on his every word. Joey and I looked at each other and clinked our bottles of beer in an unspoken victory toast. The circus had come to town. Howard Cosell was holding court.

Can't remember what Howard was going on and on about, but I do know I'd never heard the word "I" spoken so many times in one sentence. Cosell had no monitor. Cosell had no shame. It was an exercise in immodesty by a man in love with his own words. It was, however, great theater.

Joey and I were loving it when I saw Assistant Commissioner of the sports complex, Fred "Chuckles" Harrigan giving us "the evil eye." He didn't look happy, but that wasn't any standard by which you could judge Harrigan. Chuckles was never happy. He was with two other people. They were talking to Harrigan, but he wasn't listening because his eyes were fixed on us. I could see him getting more irritated moment by moment. He seemed to be turning red as he started moving towards us through the crowd like a jungle cat going in for the kill. Harrigan elbowed into our circle, standing between Joey and me.

Cosell paused, looked dismissively at Chuckles before turning back to the women and continuing his monologue.

Harrigan was out of his element. This played to our advantage. It was just in his nature to screw with people, but he didn't have any real authority in the Stadium Club and knew my uncles ran the place. He wanted to do something. I think his need to assert himself hinged on the idea, actually a correct idea, that I'd brought an uninvited guest to an ABC party. He just wasn't certain.

Harrigan's first words, sort of speaking into his hand: "Everything okay out in the lots?"

I knew he didn't give a damn about the lots but answered, "No problems, everything's cool."

Cosell stopped saying "I-something or other" and stared at us.

Chuckles, oblivious to Cosell, nodded to me.

Something was really bothering Harrigan. I sensed his target was Joey.

Cosell started back into his endless story about himself, the gaggle of good-looking women fawned obsequiously.

Harrigan gave me a meaningful look, a lot of eyebrow movement and a slight double head-bob in Kohult's direction. I felt like we were in a bad spy movie but took his gesture to be a nonverbal "Who's this guy?"

I disowned Joey, shrugging as if I had no idea.

Oblivious, Cosell droned on.

Chuckles repeated his head-bobbed question.

I shrugged again, my "No idea" nonverbal lie.

Joey was a big boy. Joey was on his own. I trusted Joey could handle anything. Chuckles would be child's play for my friend.

Harrigan, never shy, and with no reason other than he liked to screw with people, couldn't take it anymore. He turned to Joey.

"Who are you?"

Joey had no idea in the world who Harrigan was, but his instincts were perfect.

He sensed Harrigan wasn't with Nilon Brothers or ABC. Joey, his unflappable self, uttered sparks of genius. One word came out of his mouth: "Lights."

Harrigan, confused, repeated "Lights?" as a stammered question.

Joey spoke down to him, explaining patiently as if to a child. "Lights...ABC...lights, you know," gesturing above him, waving his arms, "Lights! Get it? Lights!"

Chuckles repeated "Lights" twice. First time, as moments before, like a question, then nodding pleasantly as if he saw the light and suddenly got it. "Oh yeah, Lights."

Joey smiled.

Cosell stopped talking. He looked annoyed.

The women looked confused.

Chuckles nodded uncomfortably like he understood, everything's okay, but not sure he hadn't been played.

Harrigan walked away, uncertain, uncomfortable, but not willing to call Joey out in front of Cosell who was glaring at him.

Joey nodded at Cosell, gesturing with his beer to go on.

Howard nodded back, smiled at the women and returned to his pontificating ad nauseam with "I"... yada yada yada.

After a few minutes, I turned to Joey.

"Five minutes, wander out. See you in my office."

A HUMBLE UNASSUMING MAN

As I hung up the telephone early one pleasant September afternoon, I heard a soft knock on the door to my office followed by a polite, "Excuse me." A well-dressed man in a dark gray flannel suit stood in the door with a pleasant expression on his face. It was a warm Friday afternoon in football season. The Eagles were playing somewhere out of town that weekend. I had an event at the Spectrum this night, but it was hours before any of the guys on my parking crew would be showing up. The oversized door to the large truck bay adjacent to my office was open because it was a warm Indian summer afternoon. I'd just finished washing my pickup truck, coils of hose and puddles of water everywhere. I realized the man had probably waited until I put the phone down before tapping on my door. I'd been catching up on some paperwork and making a few calls.

"Is there any way I can get into the stadium?" he asked politely.

I stood up, telling him the stadium was not open to the public and there were not many people around on a Friday afternoon. He told me Temple was practicing for a game the next day and he was with the team and needed to check on something. I let him know there would be someone in the security office under Gate B over by the Phillies Office and with the proper credentials he could get in there. He thanked me and turned to go. The man was well dressed and looked to be in his late forties, early fifties. Out of curiosity, I asked what interest he had with the team. He replied he was one of the coaches and I introduced myself, shaking his hand. His name was Wayne Hardin.

Wayne Hardin wasn't "one of the coaches," he was the head coach. I knew of Wayne Hardin; he was a coaching legend and a guy my father knew well and respected. I'd had the pleasure of meeting this man almost twenty years before while working for my father at the Navy-Marine Memorial Stadium in Annapolis when Coach Hardin had been the head football coach at The Naval Academy. It was long ago, and I'd been in high school. Nilon Brothers ran the food, drink and parking concessions at the stadium when Hardin had been coach. In fact, Nilons still did and I sent one of my crews to Annapolis for the parking operations for all their football and soccer games. I remembered Coach Hardin but had not recognized him. I did know he was currently Temple's Head Coach and had been successful in turning their program around. Hardin was a big deal. Hell, he had coached Roger the dodger Staubach at Annapolis and helped mold a Heisman Award Winner. That was a rare accomplishment to win a Heisman coming out of a military academy. Hardin coached another midshipman who received a Heisman prior to Staubach, I think it was Joe Bellino. Hardin was a good guy, great man, and an incredible coach.

We stood in the truck bay catching up. He remembered my father fondly. I told him my dad had passed away recently, and he expressed his condolences and entertained me with an amusing story about an incident involving my father and Sarge Janovich, a retired Marine who managed the Stadium in Annapolis. Hardin was a great storyteller. I could see why he and my dad had gotten along.

We had a pleasant conversation and, knowing who he was and his legitimate reason for getting into the Vet, I offered to shoot him into the Stadium through the door at the back of my truck bay that opened onto the 200-level concourse. He accepted my offer and asked if he could leave his car where he'd parked it next to my pickup truck. I cautioned him I might not be around to let him exit through the same door when he wanted to leave and how he could get back to his car. The event later at the Spectrum wouldn't involve the area where he was parked. No one would care about his car there.

I walked him into the Stadium, and we parted by the alcove that took him down through the seats and onto the field. I felt we both enjoyed that our paths had crossed again.

Back in the truck bay, I began to roll up the hose when I noticed Coach Hardin's car really could use a wash. I had everything I needed there and a little time to spare, so I washed his car before heading out to run a few errands. When I came back Coach Hardin had departed leaving nothing but a wet area where his car had been.

I was at my desk again going over some scheduling when I heard someone laughing, saying "You....it was you! You washed my car."

Coach Hardin stood in my office door, laughing and holding out a ten-dollar bill. I admitted I was the guilty party, and he insisted I take his money as he pursued me around the truck bay, laughing and telling me his side of this.

"I came back to my car and thought it had rained. I thought my car looked clean. Last thing my wife said to me as I walked out the door this morning was to remember to get our car washed before I came home. I'm driving up Broad Street almost to City Hall when it struck me it hadn't rained. What in God's name was I thinking? Not only had it not rained, but my car was in a VIP spot under cover up against the stadium and under the overhang of the concourse that ringed the building. Even if it had rained, my car couldn't have gotten wet!" Hardin was really enjoying himself having a great laugh at his own expense. We laughed ourselves silly. He had been so preoccupied with the morrow's game he had not given it much of a thought till he had gotten way up Broad. He came all the way back to pay me and tell on himself.

Coach Hardin wouldn't let it go. He insisted I take his money. I didn't want anything. I loved the guy. He was patently loveable. He said the money was well spent. A bargain: a carwash as well as a great story. I understood that last part. I took his money, telling him the money would go for a round of drinks at J.C.Dobbs later that night in his honor along with the story. He liked that angle. I knew why he and my father got along so well.

But there is one more thing. Good stories are like this.

Coach Hardin passed away in Upper Dublin in April 2017. As life and good stories will have it, I was also living in Upper Dublin at the time, but I didn't hear of his passing until later in the year. I'd known he lived nearby and had spoken to him once on the phone a few years earlier. I told whoever first answered the phone at his home to tell Coach Hardin I was the guy who washed his car at the Vet thirty-some years ago. Coach Hardin came on the phone laughing. I sent him a copy of the then unpublished manuscript of "Many Beaucoup Magics." We had fun on the phone and talked of getting together, but sadly it never came to pass. Damn.

But that's not the "One more thing."

When I heard Wayne Hardin died, I called the family to express my condolences for their loss and my family's respect for this good man. I reached one of his sons. Something I said triggered an incredible laugh, and he bellowed, "Oh my God! It was you!" Across the years Coach Hardin's son sounded just like his father the day he chased me around the parking lot garage waving a $10 bill in the air. The son told me one of his father's all-time favorite stories was about my washing his car and his dad thinking it had rained until struck by the truth driving home. His son told me his father loved to tell the story whenever the family gathered for birthdays or holidays. Everybody knew his story about the time he snuck into the Vet to check up on his team. When he came out a guy had washed his car and he thought it had rained. He was circling City Hall when he realized it had not rained, and it was crazy to not realize what happened because had been parked under cover, anyway. A good man is secure enough to laugh at himself.

The story had become a Hardin Family meme. During his eulogy at the funeral, one of his sons retold the story in his honor, saying if his father could be there himself, he'd certainly be telling it. Given that Wayne Hardin had such an incredible life, I felt honored to be a part of one of his favorite stories.

That afternoon long ago was the only time I ever spent with Wayne Hardin, but I'd always liked him. I liked him a lot more after our brief time together at The Vet.

Hey coach!

All due respect.

2½ STAR SPANGLED BANNERS

My maternal grandfather came to America from Ireland when he was 17 years old to find a better life. He came to Philadelphia with a few coins in his pocket and a scrap of paper with the name of a relative who lived in Fishtown. Mike Nilon got a job on the 23 trolley that runs up Germantown Avenue past my wife's store, Mango, in Chestnut Hill. The trolley is no longer in use, though the tracks are still there, tracing Mike's route from South Philly to the top of Chestnut Hill. It was one of the longest trolley routes in the country, over twelve miles. Mike was the low man on a crew of three that worked on his shift. The trolley ran from turn-of-the-twentieth century poverty of south Philly to the wealth of Chestnut Hill, a study in economic disparity connecting the "have nots" with the "haves." The trolley company built several amusement parks at the end of the line so the working class would have a reason to use the trolley on Sundays. Willow Grove Park and Woodside Park were two magical parks I remember going to as a child. They were places of wonder and joy. "White City," the park that had been built near Chestnut Hill in my grandfather's time, took its name from the white buildings and bandstand in the park. John Phillip Souza and Scott Joplin were some of the big name entertainment attractions who played in the parks at the far end of several trolley routes, and an unintended downside was that the have nots were being exposed to the wealth and opulence of Chestnut Hill. Sometime before World War I, a group of Hill businessmen purchased the park and shortly after a "fire" burned the park to the ground.

As White City was built, at the end of the line, it is reasonable to imagine my grandfather as a young man strolling through the park killing time during a layover. He met a little strawberry blond from Chicago. She worked in the park and lived nearby. They fell in love, married and started a family. She had come to Philadelphia because of a family tragedy. Kitty's father was one of three Irish brothers. I don't know if they were immigrants or first generation Irish, but they all worked together "on the boats" out of Chicago on Lake Michigan. One of the brothers drowned and the surviving two swore they would never go out on the Great Lakes again. Their name was Sheehan. One stayed in Chicago, finding work in the stockyards, and the other brought his family to Philadelphia because of some family connection. One descendant of that branch of the Sheehan's who remained in Chicago, 7 years younger than I, ended up in show business and you've seen the most successful member of this funny limb of the family tree, again and again and again in the movie Groundhog's Day. We have never met, though a few of my cousins have had fleeting contact with Bill Murray.

Mike and Kitty Nilon's first child, my Uncle Joe, was born in 1910 and sometime before the outbreak of WW I in Europe, my grandparents moved their growing family to Ridley Park in Delaware County. Mike, "Pop-Pop" to me, worked at Baldwin Lima Hamilton's Locomotive Works in Eddystone. I think Baldwins made tanks for the war. Turns out I also worked at Baldwin's after high school and before college and the Army 50-some years after Pop-Pop.

Mike and Kitty raised six children, four sons and two daughters, in Ridley Park. They were one of the poorest families in town, but three of their sons became multi-millionaires and built one of the most successful sports and industrial catering businesses in America. Mike Nilon's children realized their father's dream of a better life in America.

Now in his eighties, Mike Nilon, affectionately known as "Pop-Pop" worked for his sons in various capacities over the years. One of the jobs his sons created for Mike was adding two pennies to every pack of cigarettes to be sold in their vending machines. He would use a hot knife to create a slit in the cellophane cover on a pack of cigarettes so he could insert the pennies in the cover before resealing each pack with the heated knife. The purpose of this was to provide the two cents change needed when the cigarettes, which cost 28 cents, were sold in the newly invented vending machines of the early 1950s. If you are wondering why they just did not simply raise the price to 30 cents, so am I. Eventually they did, and Pop-Pop needed something else to do.

Pop-Pop was bored. A bored Pop-Pop was a problem.

In a conversation with some event organizer for The City of Philadelphia, it was mentioned they needed someone to be in the press box at JFK who could play a record of The Star-Spangled Banner on cue. It would be as a favor and a one-shot deal. The event was the Annual Police and Fireman's Hero Scholarship Thrill Show, and it was suggested that this might interest Pop-Pop. Would it be possible to have him play The Star-Spangled Banner over the loudspeaker system at the beginning of the show? It was a simple task. Someone needed to turn on the record player when the announcer on the field requested everyone to "Please stand for our National Anthem." This might give Pop-Pop something to do. Everyone was soon sorry it had ever come up.

Pop-Pop wanted to go up to the Stadium every day and rehearse. He did not drive anymore, so someone had to drive him from Ridley to Philly. He cleaned up his area, which was open air and full of pigeon droppings and worse, not having been in use for many months. He swept and cleaned, rearranged things that didn't need rearranging and thought the area he was to work in could use a little paint. A three-minute, once-in-a-lifetime gig was turning into a career. We humored him, but it was getting old, quickly.

His obsession with the project should have been a warning that there were some storm clouds on the horizon, but he was a beloved older man, and everyone thought it was kind of funny. It was just Pop-Pop being Pop-Pop. We all couldn't have been more right. We couldn't have been more wrong.

When the big day came Pop-Pop was one of the first people in the Stadium and he was dressed in a suit and tie. I cannot think of any other time I saw my grandfather in a suit and tie other than a few years later at his wake.

During early morning set up and long before the spectators arrived, it was strange to keep hearing "The National Anthem" playing over and over on the loudspeakers. Those of us working that morning did not know if they should be stocking the concession stands or removing our hats or saluting. Someone finally went up to the press box and told Pop-Pop it had to stop. He did not need to practice. A threat to take the 45-rpm record away from him till showtime settled him down.

There was a great crowd that day, perfect weather, balmy with blue skies. After a few cursory announcements, a deep baritone voice on the loudspeaker finally said, "Will everyone now stand for the playing of our National Anthem." It was Pop-Pop's cue, his big moment. He nailed it perfectly, lifting the arm on the turntable and placing it correctly on the record. Thousands of uniformed Police, Firemen and Military personnel, guests and spectators stood, turned, faced the flag, and either crisply saluted or placed their hands over their hearts.

Those familiar words boomed out of gigantic speakers everywhere, filling the air with "Oh say can you see...." the crowd smiling and singing along. It was such a beautiful day, a great cause, a Hero Scholarship Fundraiser for the children of Police and Firemen who had lost their lives in the line of duty. Everyone was in good spirits. As our National Anthem finished with the beloved words "...And the home of the Brave," a full-throated rousing cheer went up and everyone took their seats.

The moment their asses touched their seats, something unexpected happened.

Out of the loudspeakers boomed the words "Oh say can you see...." and everyone bolted to their feet again and saluted, not knowing what else to do. The song played all the way through a second time once again with everyone in uniform at attention saluting, all civilians with their hands on their hearts but with big smiles and giggles and "What the hell is going on" looks from one another. Nothing like this ever happened before, maybe anywhere, and no one knew what to do other than stand at attention and pay homage to a beloved American tradition. The cheers at the end of our anthem were louder at the end of the second rendition than for the first and everyone sat down with smiles, amused, happy in some unaccountable, indescribable way as once again their asses hit the seats.

And once again came those now much too familiar words booming out of the loudspeakers "Oh say can you see...."

And once again, everyone on their feet, this time with an exasperated groan.

What the hell is going on? Nobody knew, uncharted territory, a world of something unknown. The crowd stood. Those in uniform saluted in a ripple of suppressed laughter and confusion.

But not everyone didn't know what was going on.

We knew.

The family knew.

Oh God!

Oh No!

Pop-Pop!

Many of us were under the gun, maniacally working the job, busy as hell, preoccupied with the normal mania of the event, the unforeseen things, routine frenzy and mishaps as an event erupts. We did not pick up on the second playing of our sacred song...until someone started screaming Pop-Pop...." We knew as soon as the import of his name registered on us and took off running and screaming.

The Press Box was not easy to get to in the old JFK. From section W-O on ground level there is a free-standing fire escape with over a hundred steps, scary, precarious, flimsy...up. up..climbing shouting, cursing "Shit...piss...and corruption.." madly climbing, breathless...grunting .....up those rickety metal steps, more like an erector set than anything built with safety standards in mind, built in the 1920s almost as an afterthought. The free-standing stairs to the press box so nutso scary many who had to go up there took the longer, safer, saner way out into the Stadium and up through the spectators' seats to the top. On this day some of us went that way also. Whoever can get there first. A third Star-Spangled Banner blaring the familiar song, mocking us as we climbed and cursed. Some of Pop-Pop's colorful curses coming out of me as I ran, "Sweet suffering shit" and "Jesus H. Christ" among them.

In the stands, a stadium full of the gathered faithful saluting while grinning like children as they stood at attention, wondering, "What the hell is going on...?"

The first of us got to the Press Box and blasted into the room where the problem originated, halfway through the third rendition of The Star-Spangled Banner.

We saw our grandfather who had come to America as a young man in search of a better life with less than a dollar in change to his name in search of a better life. He sat in his chair, head in his hands, weeping, crying his heart out. He had known poverty, prejudice, hardship and pain. He had seen three of his six children become multi-millionaires. We stood looking at our sweet wonderful grandfather, the embodiment of The Great American Dream repeating over and over, "By God I love this Song....I love this country...I love America."

Oblivious to everything around him but the song, Pop- Pop wept tears of unabashed joy.

We stood there. We cried with him.

Thinking of him as I write this brings tears to my eyes all over again.

I will always miss you, Mike.

YOU'LL NEVER FIND YOUR CAR

My Uncle Jack drove a new Mercedes-Benz sports car that he parked inside the stadium during games. Nobody else had ever parked their car inside the stadium, not even the mayor. Jack parked it along the wall by his office door at the bottom of the ramp on the underground 100-level. Jack parked there and never was heard a discouraging word. This was a pure Jack move.

Pat Nilon, one of Jack's kids, was the Operations Manager for all Phillies and Eagles games. Pat was perfect for the wild west insanity of running food, drink and novelty concessions for major league sporting events. Pat was competent and unflappable. When the gates opened, and 60,000 fans streamed in, you never knew what could go wrong. There are very few businesses where you serve over 60,000 customers in a few hours. Any unforeseen problem that throws you out of whack can have serious ripple effects. This is an example of such an unforeseen occurrence.

Pat had a new Porsche. Both Jack's and Pat's cars were brown. There was just enough room for one other car along the wall outside their offices beneath the stadium where Jack had begun to park his car. Pat parked his car in front of his father's. The two cars didn't block anything and there was no problem. It just became their thing and a part of the landscape.

One day before a Phillies game Pat got to the stadium a little bit after his father. Jack's car was in its now usual spot, but in the space where Pat would normally park was a spanking new red Corvette. It was a sweetheart. It was all-star Mike Schmidt's car.

Pat went down to the Phillies locker room and asked Mike to please move his car from his parking space.

Schmitty, dressing for the game due to start shortly informed Pat it was his space. Jack Nilon had given it to him. "Got a problem; talk to Jack. I've got a game to play."

I do not think anybody raised by Jack Nilon could ever be easily intimidated. Jack's kids grew up immune to being pushed around.

Pat and Mike did a stare off. When Pat spoke, he wasn't profane. He did not raise his voice. Players in nearby locker stalls could not hear what he said. Pat told number 20 that for all he cared, Jack could give him his Mercedes-Benz if he wanted to. He could give him his house, his car, his golf clubs, his family's cat or even his own parking space, but he couldn't give him Pat's parking space because it wasn't his to give.

Schmitty had his game face on and stood toe to toe with Pat. A few players gathered around, sensing that machismo locker room thing heating up. Pat did not blink. He spoke quietly, for Mike's ears only. "In twenty minutes, your car will not be anywhere you can find it. Have a good game, but tonight you're going home to Media in a cab. You'll never find your car."

Ten minutes later, a bat boy moved Schmitty's car to the fenced-in player's lot at the top of the ramp between Gates G and H. The issue never came up again.

YOU WANTED TEN DIDN'T YOU?

Super Bowl XIV

I've only been to two Super Bowls, but they were back to back, two years in a row, and none of these stories about them have much to do with the games. My first Super Bowl was played in Pasadena, California, at the Rose Bowl in 1980, and I had never thought about going to the game until a little over a week before the game. The original plan was for Terry Tautolo and me to drive cross country together once Terry's football season came to an end. We had talked about the trip all season, but the loss to Tampa Bay only four days after Christmas came as a shock. The Eagles postseason odds to actually win Super Bowl XIV were a long shot, but nobody thought underdog Tampa Bay would run the ball 55 out of 70 snaps and send the Eagles to the showers in the first game of the playoffs. The team's charter flight got them home on the evening of the 29th only hours after the game, and I didn't get back for another day. I found Terry sitting in his apartment in Ridley Park staring at his Christmas tree, looking like his dog died. I knew he was hurting physically as well and anxious to get home. Terry told me his girl Linda, as well as his family and friends in California, had been calling to find out when he'd be home. Terry told them he didn't know because I wasn't back from Tampa yet and we were supposed to drive out together. We had planned to drive across country together once the season was over, probably sometime in mid-January. Physically and emotionally drained, he still wanted to honor his promise to me, plus he had to pack up everything in his apartment. There was a lot to do before he could head West. I told him all bets were off. "Pick up the phone, book the next flight to LAX and call Linda and tell her you'll be with her on New Year's Eve. Give me the keys to your van and the apartment and I'll see you in a couple of weeks." Once he realized it would all work out Terry gave me his Mac card to cover any unforeseen expenses closing down his apartment and getting his Van and belongings home to Long Beach. A very relieved Samoan boarded a redeye to LAX that very night.

You cannot go west without a posse and 10 days later I'm in my office at the Vet with Kevin and Pat Nilon. We are planning our trip. Pat muses "Isn't the Super Bowl in LA about the time we get out there?"

I called the Eagles' office and asked a friend of ours, Roe, if it was possible to get any tickets to the game. We were certain it was a dead-end, but what the hell. We were going out there and it was worth a try. I was prepared to have her laugh at me, but all she said was she would check it out. Roe asked how many tickets I wanted. I covered the mouthpiece on the phone and in a stage whisper hissed, "She's asking me how many tickets we want!"

Kevin said, "Four."

Pat said, "Ask for 10, maybe we'll get 4."

So, I asked Roe if we could get 10, thinking she'd flip out. Roe was cheerful, saying, "I'll check and get back to you." Stunned, I put the receiver down. We never thought we would come up with anything. Forty minutes later, the phone rang. Roe said, "I got your tickets." Anxiously I asked, "How many?" Roe, sounding a little dismayed, says, "You wanted 10, didn't you? I got you 10 tickets." The total cost of our tickets in 1980 was only $300, $30 apiece.

Today, ten tickets would cost $30,000. Pat ran upstairs and paid Roe for the tickets minutes after she put the phone down. Scalping the six extra tickets could pay for our trip.

On Friday the 11th of January 1980, my brother Kevin and I headed west in Terry's minivan with his huge TV and everything from his apartment. Our plan was to link up with Pat Nilon and another friend, Franny McKinney, at a bar in Media, have a few drinks, then hit the road for our once-in-a-lifetime trip to a Super Bowl in the Rose Bowl. The game would be played on Sunday the 20th, Steelers against the LA Rams with the Rams having a home-field advantage for the first time ever in a Super Bowl.

Our trip west started about noon on Friday and somebody saw my mother outside church on Sunday and told her she'd seen Kevin and me early Saturday morning in Media, Pennsylvania, only 4 miles away. My mother told her that must be wrong because we left around noon on Friday and must have been halfway across the country by then. My Mother was wrong; the girl was right. On Friday we only got as far as P.B. Packy's Pub in Media. Once the crowd in the bar got wind of what we were up to, they plied us with drinks, begging to go with us. With four grown men, their travel bags and everything from Terry's apartment jammed into the VW minivan, our load was dangerously far beyond any realistic capacity. We finally left the party of envious well-wishers revolving around us only because of last call and careened down State Street in Media. I was the designated driver that night, but driving the overloaded van took some getting used to. I thought the van's poor handling was from the trolley tracks in the middle of the street, but once we were out of town, I realized the overloaded van seemed to float on its tires from side to side.

My mother had trouble believing that 14 hours after we kissed her goodbye, her sons had covered only four miles.

We drove through the night, pit stops only, rolling into

Nashville just before midnight, "Saturday night Sin" blaring on the radio. We hunted for a happening bar on Beale Street. We left the bar only when they threw everybody out after last call.

Closing bars on our trip west became the status quo, with only one exception.

Sunday night we rolled into Palestine, Texas, looking to hook up with "Super Bill" Bradley at his Double B Ranch. "Soup" was out of town and no bars were open on Sundays, so we holed up in a seedy motel, got a pizza and broke into our stash of 288 one ounce bottles of hootch. The individual portions of alcohol came in two small brown, custom-made, carry-on cases embossed with "A-A" for American Airlines. Each case had twelve rows, each holding twelve tiny bottles of every imaginable liquor, 144 bottles to a case. These carry-ons had been separated, somehow, from a flight attendant. Someone at Dobbs Bar gave us the carry-ons for our trip. Looking back on this, I can't rationalize accepting the drinks, but they sure came in handy later when gunfire ripped up the night.

Entertainment in Palestine was provided by a local maniac in a pickup truck firing a gun, driving at breakneck speed, ringing the motel in swirls of dust and gun shots while screaming for his wife. Suddenly a motel room with a back door made perfect sense. Last call in Palestine was up to us. We checked out early.

On Monday night we closed another bar in Dallas.

Tuesday night we closed a bar in Winslow, Arizona. That's where our trip took a bizarre turn. The next bar we closed would be one we couldn't drive to but would have to walk. It would be over 7 miles from where we parked our van.

In the last days planning for our trip, and by planning I'm not referring to any adult or practical considerations, I thought it would be a good idea to spend one night of our Westering movement at the Phantom Ranch at the bottom of the Grand Canyon. I'd read about the Phantom Ranch once in National Geographic but never thought I'd get there until I realized it was on our route, well sort of on our route. I made the arrangements before we left and discovered for only twenty-five dollars each, we could have reservations for a bunk and two meals at The Phantom Ranch.

We arrived at the Lodge on the South rim of the Grand Canyon at 9 am Wednesday morning. The weather prediction on the radio was for snow. The concierge issued us four prepaid receipts to present when we got to the ranch at the bottom. Snow flurries swirled around us as we left the lodge.

There are two trails on the South rim leading down to The Phantom Ranch. The Bright Angel Trail, with its trailhead closest to the big lodge in Grand Canyon Village is a much longer trek, close to 13 miles, and not nearly as steep as the South Kaibab Trail which is a little more than half the distance, but extremely steep. Both trails have an almost one-mile vertical drop from the South rim around 7000 feet to the Colorado River on the bottom at 2400 feet. From researching the trails, our plan was to go into the canyon on the Kaibab and climb out on the Bright Angel known to be a much easier hike. As we drove from the Lodge, several miles away to a parking area near the top of the Kaibab, the snowfall increased, no longer flurries.

We planned to travel light. I had a jungle rucksack containing two large canteens of water, four pairs of socks, rolling papers, some pot, wooden matches, two six-packs of beer, forty-something little bottles of assorted booze courtesy of American Airlines, two emergency flares, a survival knife and a whistle.

We locked the van and walked to the edge of the South rim. There was a foot of snow on the ground from previous snowfalls, and snow falling around us intensified dramatically. Visibility, as we began our descent into the canyon, less than 15 feet, a "white-out." We not only couldn't see the North rim on the other side of the canyon, we couldn't even see down into the canyon in front of us, only a narrow trail hugging a cliff wall dropping off on one side into whiteness and God knows what. We debated turning around and getting a room at The Grand Lodge. Wisdom and logic overruled by a sense that this was our only shot, maybe ever, to go down into the canyon. It remains one of the most foolish, and yet better, decisions I have ever made. One of our guys said, "The road to the Super Bowl is that way" and pointed down into the canyon. I'm thinking of "The Donner Pass."

We plowed into the white wall, unable to see ten feet in front of us or to either side. One of the most remarkably haunting images I have ever experienced appeared an hour or so into our descent down the canyon wall. We were inching our way down a ridge line, the vaguely defined trail, about 4 feet wide, dropping off steeply into dense white on both sides. We walked in muted silence, the falling snow absorbing sound. In the distance, there was an unusual sound, so out of place, we couldn't grasp what we were hearing until we started asking each other if they heard it also. It had to be a bell of some sort, but the acoustics of the silencing snow gave it a feathered tone as it muted through the snow. The sound coming up the ridge line slowly toward us. Our descent on this part of the trail was very steep, acutely uncomfortable with not being able to see on either side what was hidden by the falling snow. I was on point and saw it first, an apparition coming out of the mist. At first it was undefined but as it came closer, bringing the sound of the bell with it, we saw a park ranger atop a mule leading maybe eight mules roped in line together lumbering up the trail. On both sides of each animal were fastened large canvas bags of trash from the bottom of the canyon. We later learned that this was the only way refuse from the Phantom Ranch was brought out. We stood aside on the edge of the trail watching this ghostlike mule train pass us, disappearing up the trail into the misty white. When the mule train disappeared, the fading sound of the bells lingered. The memory of that passing is as strong today as it was then.

Snow stopped after an hour or so. Sun came out and burned the mist out of the canyon. We could see everything around us. To look at the Grand Canyon in a photograph or from the rim is one thing, but when the sun cleared away the mist and visibility jumped from only a few feet to over half a mile, looking down into this national treasure, the view was so spectacular; we stood there looking back at the path we had come down in stunned amazement.

About an hour later and maybe halfway to the ranch, there was a lookout point at a "U-shaped bend" in the trail. We took one of our first breaks. We were drinking beers and passing a joint, taking it all in. Moments before, after looking at all the colored strata of rock, I'd said something about wishing I'd gotten a book on the canyon's geology because it seemed as if we were descending backwards in time through rock formations millions of years old. We had no appreciation of what we were looking at.

There is a saying: "When you need a teacher, one will appear." The lookout where we dangled our feet over the edge was adjacent to a blind turn in the rock wall. As soon as I made my comment about geology Paul McNee walked into our lives. He bopped around the blind turn and stood looking at us, dressed as if he'd just stepped out of the pages of L.L. Bean's catalog, dressed for hiking the canyon. He had brilliantly colored clothing, bright reds and yellows and a sensible purple backpack with the perfect boots for a trek in the canyon.

We stared at him.

Someone offered him something to drink. Paul had an infectious laugh. Everyone was smiling when he spoke. His words seasoned by his appealing Aussie accent. "Fair dinkum, mates. What luck, I bump into a pack of pistol prick Yanks hanging off a wall in the canyon.

First thing they do is offer me a drink. What a'ya got?"

We played with that one back and forth for a while, us saying "What do you want"? Him asking what we had. Came down to Paul saying, "Well, you can't have everything. I mean, here we are halfway down the bleeding Grand Canyon...." His argument trailed off as if he'd made an irrefutable point, so I jiggled my rucksack filled with dozens of clinking little glass bottles and we made a believer out of him.

Paul was from Sydney, Australia, said he taught school. I asked what he was doing over here during the school year. He said, "Down Under, its summer, Mate." Told us he's traveling around studying several American canyons. I asked what he taught. He said, "Science, geology," pointing backwards with his thumb, "you know, rocks."

I said, "You want to go to the Super Bowl with us?"

Paul smiled, asking, "Are ya gay?" Not exactly the response I'd expected.

I told him "No, not a big deal one way or another" and before any of this could sink in, he fired off another non sequitur.

"Are you Moonies?"

I'm having second thoughts about having invited him to the Super Bowl, but laughed, telling him we weren't Moonies either. Why the questions?

Paul said he landed in San Francisco and everybody who was nice to him and wanted him to go home with them was either gay or a Moonie.

We sat there drinking, smoking, and laughing our asses off before we headed down hill together.

The trail to the bottom was built in the 1920s and at the bottom a short tunnel cut through rock walls opening onto a narrow suspension bridge across the Colorado River.

On the eastern side of the Colorado at a confluence with the Bright Angel Creek, sits The Phantom Ranch. For that unbelievable bargain price of only twenty-five dollars we had a small log cabin with two sets of bunk beds, heat, bedding, electricity, cold running water and a toilet. Showers with hot water were nearby in a much larger log cabin. Dinner that evening and breakfast the next day would be served to overnight residents as part of our package deal. These accommodations were why we hadn't backpacked sleeping bags or a tent.

The meals were incredible. One generous portion of steak, baked potato, vegetables, freshly baked bread, coffee and dessert. Seconds while they lasted were available with the only exception being steak. The Ranch staff served cold beer and wine for an additional charge; I think Coors long necks were a very reasonable ninety cents. Nobody ordered wine, so I forget what it cost, but it wasn't much. After dinner when the tables had been cleared they kept the canteen open until 11 PM, so once again at the bottom of the Grand Canyon we managed to drink until last call then went back to our cabin, opened our rucksack bar and played cards. Paul had a sleeping bag and slept on the floor.

Breakfast the following morning was generous, pretty much all you could eat again if provisions lasted. The food was plentiful, and we were ravenous. Pancakes, home fries, scrambled eggs, sausage and bacon and toasted muffins but the biggest surprise on the floor of the Grand Canyon occurred during our meal when I saw a tiny little hand with pointed claws push aside a round metal disc on the cabin wall nearby. The round cover was a makeshift solution to a hole in the wall from an old stovepipe and the hole just a little smaller than the 9" cover. The disc was held in place with one nail top center on the circle. The cover could swing side to side. I first noticed a slight movement; it caught my attention because the little disk began swinging slightly side to side. I had a mouthful of scrambled eggs. I stopped chewing and stared at the disk. A little hand came out, pushing the circle aside so we could see each other. It was a raccoon, a baby raccoon. We watched each other all through breakfast. I've never had a more whimsically pleasant time during a meal, ever.

After breakfast we strolled along the banks of Bright Angel Creek looking for the tail end of the Bright Angel trail. The Bright Angel was almost twice as long as the Kaibob Trail we came down on. I hoped this meant the Bright Angel was only half as steep. It was, but it didn't matter. The trail kicked our asses. "Half as steep" my red Irish ass. The hike to the rim was exhausting, but we made it out by sunset and there are only a few things in the physical realm more satisfying than the taste of a cold beer while sitting down at a table after having just climbed out of that "Mama Jamma": The Grand Canyon.

We made it back to the same bar in Winslow, Arizona we'd been in two nights earlier, about three hours before last call, and crossed the California Border on Friday morning as the sun came up, just another tequila sunrise.

We had made last call every night on the road except in Palestine, Texas, where the bars closed on Sundays but somebody shot up the place.

Paul McNee from Sydney, Australia, came with us. To this day Paul has a ticket stub from the Super Bowl and an incredible story to go with it.

We are mates for life.

YO, "JUICE"

Super Bowl XIV

Super Bowl Sunday, January 20th, 1980, the Rams faced off with the Steelers in Pasadena, California, to play in The Rose Bowl beneath cloudless blue skies. The day a mild 74 degrees. On the way to the game, McNee kept looking at his ticket. Paul asked me if he could keep the ticket stub as a souvenir. I told him, no problem, it belonged to him.

He sighed in relief, saying, "When I get home nobody will believe me when I tell them I met a bunch of yanks hanging off a wall in the Grand Canyon with a fully stocked bar, and they took me to The Super Bowl.

We not only didn't make any money scalping the five tickets we had left, we almost had to eat one, unloading it at the very last minute for $30 as we were about to go through the turnstiles.

Something weird occurred just before we went into the Stadium. The incident involved my brother Kevin and O. J. Simpson. Simpson was simply trying to get into the game, but a big part of him was enjoying the hell out of the large crowd of fans begging for his autograph. By his side was a beautiful young California girl whom he would one day marry and another day brutally murder.

But this was Sunday, 20 January 1980, and no one can ever know what lies ahead.

Simpson was signing no autographs, trying to get away from the crowd and into the Stadium. Kevin yelled at him.

"Yo! Juice, bet you'll sign this one!"

Kevin held out the baseball cap he was wearing and a pen.

Simpson looked at the hat. He looked at Kevin.

Simpson smiled, took the hat and pen, and scrawled something on the brim saying, "I'll sign this one!"

Okay, humor me here. A little game, so to speak. What would make Simpson hurrying to a super box and the celebrity-worshiping circus awaiting him, pause to sign this hat? Why would Simpson stop to sign only Kevin's hat?

What was it with Kevin's hat?

I'm not going to tell you for a while. I want you to think about that hat.

WHAT KIND OF CRITTERS YA GOT?

Superbowl XIV

When we were in LA for the Super Bowl, we stayed at Terry Tautolo's house and the entire week was a 24/7 party. Late in the week the three amigos I was traveling with and Terry decided they were going to take a trip to Lake Tahoe in the van. After traveling across the country in that deathtrap, I had no interest in the excursion. They would be gone several days, so I decided I would ride Terry's bike down to the ferry and head out to Catalina Island overnight.

I arrived on the island in the early afternoon in the little harbor town of Avalon and cruised around on the bike exploring until I found a room in what had once been the home of Zane Gray, an American writer of novels of the old West. In the evening, I went downtown, had a great dinner all by myself, and then sat at the bar for a while soaking up some local lore. It was a good evening up till then, and I was happy with my decision not to climb back in the van for any more of the baja we had been on crossing the country. I took a walk as it turned dark and smoked a joint as I walked up a narrow road that went alongside a golf course. There was a half-moon with visibility coming and going as the moon played in and out of patches of clouds. Being on an island with no industry 21 miles off the coast of California, there were times when I knew I'd never seen so many stars in the sky. After a great dinner, a couple of drinks, and a joint, I was feeling a great sense of peace. After a while, the road was no longer paved. The lights of houses to my right became less frequent, and the road ahead seemed darker as the moon moved behind the clouds. I felt safe and comfortable and was thoroughly enjoying my Catalina experience.

I heard it before I saw it. I didn't know what it was, but I stopped and stood perfectly still in a way I hadn't frozen in place since my time on the Cambodian border. I knew something was wrong, and that I was in extreme danger. I turned my head to my left where the golf course had been. It took me almost a half-minute to turn my head. If you had been watching me, you would have had difficulty knowing that I was moving at all. Within 15 feet of me was the largest animal I had ever seen that wasn't in a zoo. Partly obscured by some shrubbery between us, it wasn't that I couldn't tell what it was, but it was that I couldn't believe what I thought it was. It was larger than a Volkswagen beetle and facing the same direction as me and looking straight ahead, but I knew two things. There was nothing between us, but a few bushes and it was extremely disturbed I was there. I knew I hadn't crossed any fences or gone into a restricted area, but realized I was in extreme danger. I felt like I had stumbled into some Hollywood horror movie. The animal was pawing the earth with its front hoofs and snorting angrily at the ground. I took a step backwards. It must've taken me a minute to move that one foot. The animal snorted and continued to paw the ground. I thought it must have weighed at least 700 pounds. Another minute and I moved another foot backwards. I did not turn around; I just kept moving one foot after another, imperceptibly slowly, step by step back the way I had unfortunately come. The animal wasn't appeased in any way, and I wasn't feeling any better about this. I must've moved about 25 yards backwards over the next 5 to 10 minutes. I hadn't turned around, nor had the animal. It just kept snorting from lungs probably larger than me, pawing the ground angrily, letting me know I didn't belong there. It did not like me at all. I had fallen from a state of wonder and bliss to one of abject terror and a feeling I must be losing my mind in the few seconds since I heard that first horrific snort. The only thing working for me was that as I backed up ever so slowly, the beast had not turned around and come after me.

I wasn't about to turn around and have it behind me, so I continued to walk backwards almost 50 yards. I turned around slowly, moving away from it as quickly as I dared, and I'm telling you I didn't dare much. I was terrified and so was anything else nearby because every living thing had become graveyard quiet in deference to whatever that beast, angrily snorting and pawing the ground might be. When I got down the road at least 100 yards, I started to run for my life. I ran all the way back into town past the golf course. I ran through the pain. When I got back to the bar in the restaurant where I'd had dinner, I was breathless and weak.

The bartender remembered me by name and smiled when I ordered a beer and a double shot of Jack Daniels. Not realizing how perceptive he was, he smiled when he said, "You look like you've seen a ghost." I tossed the Jack back and took a long pull of my beer. The bartender looked at me curiously when I asked him, "What kind of critters you got on this Island?"

He named the normal animals you might expect, all the way down to dogs and cats until he finally said the one word that pulled me back from the edge, reassuring me, I hadn't gone crazy. He said they have wild buffalo up in the hills on Catalina Island and sometimes in the morning, they'd wander down out of the hills. The police would have to herd them off the beach and back into the hills. I was not crazy. That was a God dammed 700-pound wild buffalo I'd run into. He was matter of fact about it; the locals were used to visits. Nobody got hurt, but occasionally a few cars or fences got damaged. I sat there for the next few hours drinking myself into a coma.

It turned out I could blame the heirs to the Wrigley Chewing Gum fortune for my run-in with the buffalo. In the '30s they thought buffalo would be a great addition for their estate up in the hills and had introduced them to Catalina Island, where they roamed without a discouraging word and happily multiplied ever since.

I went back to Long Beach on the ferry the next day.

I don't think I've ever seen a buffalo since.

KEVIN'S HAT

Super Bowl XIV

The baseball hat Kevin wore to the Super Bowl XIV in Los Angeles belonged to Terry Tautolo. It had the symbol of a football on the front of the cap with the letters "NFLPA" forming the football logo for the NFL Players Association, which was the union that protected the players' rights and had given them their pensions. I do not know where that hat is today and whatever it might be worth with Simpson's signature, but it's nothing I would want to have.

I dangled the hat in front of you to make a point. I do not know where my good friend Terry Tautolo is right now, or even if he is still alive. Terry has suffered grievously from his time in the NFL and the years of brain-damaging violent contact no football helmet could ever have prevented. Terry does not blame football or the NFL in any way for any neurological issues he might have. He chose not to enter into the lawsuit with other former players against any of his employers or the teams he has played for. To his extreme credit, his former coach at UCLA and the Philadelphia Eagles, Dick Vermeil, somehow found that Terry had fallen on hard times several years ago and stepped in and helped Terry to get back on his feet. I spoke to Terry at the time but have since lost contact and have no way of knowing where he is or how he is doing. I can only say Coach Vermeil's aid was considerable and effective at the time.

CROWN ROYAL HAS TO GO?

Super Bowl XV

This is another Super Bowl story that has nothing to do with the game as "Crown Royal's Gotta Go?" relates to something that transpired after Philadelphia's 27-10 loss as the sun came down on our dream season. Everybody I was with at the game in New Orleans went off to deal with our Super Bowl loss in their own way. Somehow, we all got separated for most of the night. For us, The City that care forgot became a place for people who just needed time by themselves.

My brother Kevin ended up at O'Brien's, famous for their signature drink, "The Hurricane" as well as their immense jungle-like outdoor patio with tables often hidden in the dramatically tangled vegetation of giant tropical plants. It was a good place to avoid people. Kevin settled in, ordering a Heineken and a double shot of Crown Royal. His waiter said, "Whoa, you're the man," smiling approvingly at Kevin's choice. The waiter was setting up for the crush of people heading his way after the game. Kevin had worked in the bar and restaurant business for a long time. He introduced himself to the waiter, whose name was Andre, offering to buy him a double Royal and a "Heiney." Andre could leave his drinks on Kevin's table, well secluded, deep in the garden, out of sight. Andre was welcome, whenever he had any breaks in the action, to stop by for a taste. Andre had just come on shift for the evening. It was going to be a wild night. Andre was up for a good time. He came back promptly with two Heinekens and four generously poured Crown Royals. No one was anywhere around them to hear the clink of their glasses as they toasted the Eagles.

Andre was getting busy, so he slipped away. But from time to time, he snuck back into the high ferns to visit Kevin for a little nip.

The patio started to get crowded. Andre's night heating up.

A wild throng of unusually rowdy men, even by French Quarter standards, had gathered around a large table just off Kevin's right. They didn't sound as if they were upset with the results of the game. Another table off in the bushes to Kevin's left had drawn another hard drinking "Wild Bunch." The night was getting intense; Kevin quickly recognized a lot of men in his vicinity wearing blue ice bags with white polka dots, ace bandaged on the outside of their Levi's. They wore them as a badge of honor, which in a way they were. White polka dots were everywhere. He knew what the ice bags meant from hanging out with Eagles after games. These men were ball players. These men were the Oakland Raiders. Someone in the locker room must've yelled, "Meet up at O'Brien's before we sack this town."

Kevin had retreated into the bushes to console himself, only to have the extreme misfortune of landing in the middle of the Oakland Raiders as they gathered to howl at the moon. Raiders and their entourage passed Kevin's table occasionally, taking casual note of an unhappy guy in full Eagles regalia nursing drinks by himself back in the ferns. Nobody said anything to him or bothered Kevin in any way. Kevin was a "never mind."

An hour went by. O'Brien's was on fire, tiki torches and laughter everywhere. It seemed to Kevin that almost the entire Oakland Raiders team was scattered about at tables all around him and their night was starting to take off. Kevin sat there in an ill-fitting, borrowed and soiled ultra-suede sport coat with cigarette burns on the sleeve, an oversized silver wing attached with Velcro on his bicep. Kevin, a study of dejection, the polar opposite of everyone near him. Mother's cautioned children: "Don't go near that man." Proudly wearing his Eagles hat, nobody spoke so much as a word to Kevin.

Things changed quickly.

A beautiful woman in Raiders colors wore an outfit leaving little to the imagination. Several ballplayers were all over her. To most of the men, she was remarkably attractive, flirtatious, and available. To Kevin, she was a high maintenance mannequin, dead set on getting her own way and nothing but trouble. Kevin's radar put him on high alert. In her, Kevin correctly sensed a major shift in his fortune.

The woman tapped a glass with a spoon to get everyone's attention, announcing she wanted a team photo on this momentous occasion.

In the largest clearing in that part of the garden, Kevin sat alone at his table. The woman dragged players from the right and left, forming a group gathered around and behind Kevin, who continued sipping his drink in silence. It might have gone off okay, but the woman, framing her memorable keepsake, looked through her viewfinder and discovered Kevin in full Eagles regalia in the middle of her grouping. The woman screamed, "That man cannot be in my picture! He has got to go." She stamped her pretty feet. Kevin raised a glass in salute and to his eternal credit said, "I'm not going anywhere."

Maybe they were just a block off Bourbon Street, but in many ways, they were out in the jungle. Raiders started looking around for some place to toss Kevin. Vegas odds would have favored Kevin was headed for a dumpster. Smart money would have bet on the dumpster.

At that very moment, Andre, a tray full of drinks held high, came out of the bushes to the right. As the only link to anyone on O'Brien's staff, Andre became the court of final appeal. The woman called out, "Waiter, waiter...." She gains Andre's attention, she pouts, flicking her finger towards Kevin contemptuously, demanding "That... that man, he's got to go. He can't be in my picture."

Andre looks around, trying to figure out what is going on. He looks at Kevin who points to the drink in his hand, raises his glass and asks, "Crown Royal's got to go?"

Andre raises his tray high above his head, spinning theatrically, saying for all to hear as he moves off smartly into the ferns: "He stays. Crown Royal is in the picture." Andre has spoken. Andre is gone. Kevin sips Royal through a shit-eating grin. The Great Oz has spoken. Case closed.

The whole posing for the picture production had been quite a digressive buzzkill. Grumblings grew. "Take the damn picture. Let's get the hell out of here." These guys had just won the biggest contest of their lives and were ready to howl.

The woman wasn't happy. Running out of time and options, she had no choice.

The woman snapped the picture.

Somewhere out there in the cosmos is an exceedingly rare team photo of the Oakland Raiders taken on the night they won the Super Bowl. The team is huddled around Kevin in the lush gardens of O'Brien's. The lighting and focus are "picture perfect." Kevin is the default centerpiece in the photo. In his Eagles hat with the Silver Eagles wing on his sleeve, he looks and is both drunk and seedy. But it is what happened in the nanosecond before the flash of the camera that mattered most. Kevin's eyes are crossed, and some frothy dark bile is visibly drooling onto his shirt. Kevin's tongue is sticking out of his mouth to one side as far as possible and the forefinger of one hand is pushed up into his nose past the first knuckle. It looks as if he is having a stroke but enjoying it. Kevin's other hand is raising a shot glass in salute.

Philadelphia lost the game but won the after-party.

Andre saved the day with his ruling: "He stays; Crown Royal is in the picture!"

If there is a moral to this story, here it is, "Respect your servers, and they will respect you back."

Kevin left Andre an incredible tip that night. I am fairly sure Andre thinks of Kevin every time someone orders Crown Royal.

I know I do.

A DAY AT THE BEACH

There were five of them, full of life, young and strong as wild horses. It was a warm afternoon in early June. In the fall they would go their separate ways, off to colleges scattered all around the country, two on athletic scholarships for football. All but one of them had played together as varsity standouts on a local high school team. They took their team to the next to final round of the playoffs. Locally these kids were hot shit. Today they were tossing around a battered football on the beach in Ocean City, New Jersey.

It was good to be young and vibrantly alive.

The wind, constant but mild, and the beach had few sunbathers scattered about, giving the boys plenty of room to run free. Wild horses need to run free.

Not far from where they were working out, three men sat on the beach, minding their own business, just hanging out. They were "shooebies," having driven down from Philly to sit on the beach for a few hours and look at the ocean. They hadn't brought much with them: no chairs, umbrella, or anything like that. Two had towels, one lay in the sand. To the kids they looked to be "old guys," probably in their thirties. They'd driven down from Philadelphia on a whim to sit by the ocean on what the weatherman predicted might be the nicest day of the year so far. And so far, the weather report seemed exactly right. "What is so rare as a day in June?"

The kids threw an impressively long pass. The ball caught a renegade gust of wind, escaped extended arms and fingertips, landing in a spray of sand at the feet of the old guys. One of the kids jogged over to get the ball. He apologized politely, sincere, picking up the old football.

Older guy closest to him, says, "Wanna have a little game?"

"Sure, love to, we can choose up sides."

"Nah, we'll just play you guys. Us 'gainst y'all, that'll work." The old guy had a Texas accent.

"There's five of us, only three of you."

The local kid's friends had come up, gathering around. Everybody stood around, taking stock of each other. The men, easily 6 feet tall, one a little taller, and all three in decent shape, for their age. The kids, roughly that size, were in their prime. What the hell were these old guys thinking?

One of the local kids said they'd flip a coin; older guy with the east Texas drawl told 'em no need, he'd kick off.

Three guys against five and they're gonna kick off first.

Moving back up the beach to receive, one of the kids said, "Let's really kick their sorry asses. Show 'em who we are. Not havin' this in our house."

Things went south on the kickoff. The local kids had played a lot of ball. They'd all fielded punts since they were little kids. Nothing prepared them for what happened. "Super Bill" Bradley owns to this day the record for the longest punt in a game at the University of Texas, 72 yards. Hard to believe anyone will ever take that one away from him.

Billy tee'd off. He boomed one. It went up and up and the kids craned their necks and their mouths fell open. The ball arched thirty yards behind where the five kids waited to receive the ball, their mouths forming wide open gaping "O's" making them look like fish. One of them ran back, grabbed it, and started up the field. Didn't get far; the three men were all over him. The old guys could move. It was on.

Their first pass was batted down.

The second pass was intercepted by Bill "Soup," only two years out of pro ball and holder of an NFL record for most interceptions in the league two years in a row. Billy came out of nowhere, and because he did, no one touched him as he took it to the house. Old guys passed for two, the score eight to zero. For the local kids, it never got much better than that. For the three guys from Philly, it never got any worse.

All three of the old guys passed the ball at one time or another. Billy jabbered nerve-rattling cat calls and coded audibles all day long. Ozzie made incredible leaping saves, and every time a cluster of guys went high in the air, he came down with it. The third guy on their team was my brother Jimmy, no athletic slouch by any means. At six- two and hard as oak, Jimmy lettered in football, lacrosse, and hockey for four years at Norwich University in Vermont and has been inducted into Norwich's Hall of Fame. Jimmy had also been the Director of Freddy Shero's summer hockey camp in Valley Forge for the last three of its' four-year run. Both Ozzie and Billy led their high school football teams to win Texas State Football Championships, different years, the same battered trail to the prize. Ozzie's teammate at Lee High School in San Antonio had been Tommy Cramer, currently starting QB for The Minnesota Vikings. When Oz didn't come down with the ball, Jimmy or Billy did. The game wasn't a shutout; the kids got some rhythm, but it was a good-natured rout: scorched earth, burning sand.

The kids caught on pretty soon. It was a beautiful day by the ocean, and there were no cheap shots nor animosity. The turnaround from what they thought was going to happen to what unfolded came as a total surprise to them, an unexpected clinic in sandlot football as the five "grasshoppers" realized they'd met their masters. There was a time mid-game when in their huddle, there was a lot of panicked "Who the hell are these guys?" but the kids came full circle with the experience and embraced the moment.

The game ended on a positive note, even though the old guys took the day. As they shook hands, one of the kids said, "So are you going to tell us who you really are?" Turned out they knew both Ozzie and Billy and had seen them play. They were both star-struck and gob smacked. One of the kids ran up to his house nearby, coming back with an ice bucket full of beers and a magic marker. They drank the beer, asked a million questions, and listened to stories on end. They all signed the football.

Somewhere in south Jersey, there's an old battered football with eight names scrawled on it and a hell of a story to go with it if anybody bothers to ask.

TOM GARVEY, VET STADIUM, 19148

It wasn't a big deal, but I loved the idea that mail could reach me in the stadium addressed only with my name, The Vet, and our zip code.

Charlie worked for the post office in the 19148 area, and both the Vet and the Spectrum were on his route. In the Vet, Charlie did not have that many stops. On the fourth floor, he would have the Commissioner of Parks and Recreation and city offices right next door to the Eagles' front office. On the ground level, he'd have the Sixers and the Phillies front offices and underground on the 100-level, the Nilon Brothers concession offices. I enjoyed running into Charlie around the building from time to time, and he knew I worked for Nilons.

Once any mail for me ended up in Charlie's mailbag, he knew to leave it with Kathy, Nilon's receptionist downstairs.

Getting mail like that made me feel at home, which is what I came to believe the Vet was.

SOUTHERN WIND

You have probably never wondered where the elephants had been for the last six weeks before the circus came to town each year in early June. That probably indicates you're a little saner than if you had wondered about things like that. Either way, I will tell you.

I was sitting on the curb just off Pattison Avenue trying to write a poem. I was the "early man" that day. Phillies to play San Diego at 7:05 that night. It was a little after 2:30 in the afternoon, and cars for tonight's game would come in dribs and drabs when they started arriving. I didn't mind sitting on the curb and having time to read or write, but I hated charging the earliest arrivals. They were always people who worked at the games, and their only alternative was to park far away if they could find a space. The City of Philadelphia got 85% of the revenue, and they counted the cars every night. So back in the days when I first worked in the lot as a cashier supervisor, I was known as the "early man." For the first few hours, I would only collect parking fees from a few dozen cars, but the city required one gate had to be open so no one could sneak in early. Anyone coming that early almost always was there to work at the game, and two dollars was a big chunk of what they would earn. I hated to charge them, but City Hall tasked a man from L & I, Licenses and Inspections, to count any cars in the lots when we opened and again at the end of the night, so I had no choice.

The only gate coming off Pattison Avenue opens onto the north lot. The Vet sat on ground, mostly blacktop, roughly the size of thirty-something football fields bordered by Broad Street, Pattison Avenue, 10th Street, and Packer Avenue. Across the street on the northeastern corner of the North lot at the intersection of 10th and Packer, almost a quarter mile from the gate off Pattison, sat a ten-story hotel. In the ripples of heat off the sunbaked blacktop, the image of the hotel wavered in a blur, so it looked like a mirage. For me, it was.

I've always wanted to be a writer. I almost didn't have a choice. Life gave me great stories. I've never had to make anything up. If anything, I'm more of a "Storyteller" than a disciplined and prolific writer. It is exceedingly difficult for me to write. I stare at a blank page of paper in horror. It took me almost 47 years and well over 10,000 hours to publish Many Beaucoup Magics and to me, it will never be exactly the way I want it.

Writing nags my Irish soul. Dreams have a price.

The hotel on the farthest corner of almost 40 acres of blacktop rippled in undulating waves of summer heat. It really did look like a mirage. The longest running writers' conference in America, the Philadelphia Writers' Conference, founded in 1949, was scheduled to offer workshops, classes and contests in late June. The conference was grounded in the belief that writers gain from fellowship with other writers. It would be held in the hotel I could see shimmering in the heat waves from where I sat working on a poem. Synchronicity, kismet, fate, whatever, it was meant that I should go there. I had enrolled in several workshops and looked forward to the lectures as well as hanging out with writers. I was desperate for anything that might motivate me, cranking my battery to write. It would be my first experience of this kind.

I was jazzed.

Information provided in a brochure outlined workshops and

discussion groups available. I signed up for short story, novel, and poetry. The poetry workshop requested submission of a poem to be judged for consideration of a prize to be given at the closing ceremonies banquet on Sunday evening.

So, I felt I had to come up with a new poem for the conference, something special. I'd written a few poems over the years, but I wanted to use the poetry workshop's submission requirement to motivate me to write something both new and better. If that doesn't make much sense, remember I'm the guy who wondered where the elephants had been hanging out before they came to Philly.

So, I'm sitting on the curb at Pattison at the Vet with a clipboard and a quandary. I'm trying to write. I close my eyes. I take a deep, relaxing breath. I go inside myself to "where my meanings are" seeking ways to meld emotions and feelings into images that will live. I feel a refreshing breeze that brings a gagging stench. It makes me hold my breath.

The elephants had been in the bowels of Madison Square Garden, six basement levels beneath street level in Manhattan, for a six-week gig before riding the circus train to Philly. The circus performed two or three shows daily with every seventh day dark so the performers could have a night off.

The poor elephants didn't have a union. They never got outside in Manhattan even once. I have it on the absolute best authority that for their six miserable weeks in the Garden, the elephants did not relieve themselves with anything close to regularity. Elephant feces has a volume of 20 liters, nearly a thousand times more than dogs. Traumatized by their underground environment, they saved it all up for Philly.

In Philly, the elephants let it fly. I am sitting in the sun on a curb trying to write a poem, downwind from the elephants on the corner across the street. The circus set up a compound of tents and trucks at the top of the only ramp down into the Spectrum's

141

underground on the East side of the building. The circus area took up the S-1 South parking lot by the truck ramp on the corner of 11th and Pattison, not far from my gate across the street. I was in a classic "lose-lose situation." If there was no wind, it meant much greater heat as there were no trees or shade where I had to be. If there was any hint of a cooling breeze, it meant the elephants sent their foul-smelling calling cards. Either way, nothing poetic was coming my way. I stared at a blank page; my eyes burned.

When the wind blew a certain way, it was almost as though the air was greasy with a green haze that made my eyes go dry. Hell might not be a place of fire, but maybe something more like the parking garage the elephants recently came from deep beneath Madison Square Garden. The elephant's situation in the S-1 lot at the Spectrum was only a little better, though in open air, but with six weeks of elephant dung exploding in the noonday sun, any improvement over conditions in the garden was lost on me.

I could not breathe.

I didn't get any writing done.

The writers' Conference was two days away. I had nothing but a blank page and dry, red, and swollen eyes.

I was falling asleep at home that night when the words "Long home from that journey" came to me. I kept repeating these words to myself, worried I might not remember them. Extremely tired, I couldn't take the chance. I got out of bed, rummaged around, and wrote the line on the back of a used envelope. I went to sleep.

The next day as the early man I sat on the curb, made my peace with the elephants as best I could, and built on the five words salvaged from the edge of sleep. "Southern Wind," a title I came up with, is an allusion to a line from Shakespeare's "Hamlet." Elizabethans believed madness came with winds from the bitterly cold Northwest, much as many today believe a full moon courts odd behavior. The line from "Hamlet,": "I am mad but North-north-west, when the wind is southerly, I know a hawk from a handsaw" is at play in "Southern Wind." I'm haunted by the elusive book I longed to write about Vietnam. How to tell a story about my generation's war without either romanticizing or glorifying the debacle that crushed life's greatest joy from the mothers of so many friends killed in Vietnam? From this need in me came my poem "Southern Wind." The poem can speak for itself, and shortly it will.

The Conference became a calming placebo. The interactions, discussions, sharing of frustrations, and ideas were all good for me. At the last minute, I took my mother as my date to the awards banquet. A woman I'd been dating couldn't make it. My mother wanted to go and meet writers.

The last award of the night was for poetry. Third, then second-place awards were announced. The winners shuffled out of their seats, took their awards, and sat down.

In my poetry class, and there were several other sections, there was an electrifying aesthetic poet from New York. He owned a popular restaurant in the Hamptons. This established poet was as brilliant as he was a decent guy and considered to be a shoo-in for first prize. He had earned his juice and wore it well.

When the hostess said, "And for Southern Wind..." my mother stood up and screamed. Nothing subtle here, hardly an indoor scream, more a 700-level at the Vet, scream. I was smiling, laughing, and self-consciously bumbling my way to the stage. My mother, spinning in her chair, was telling anybody she made eye contact with, "That's my Tommy! He's going to be a writer."

Was I embarrassed? Not a bit. It was a little awkward, but she was my mother. That night became one of my greatest memories with her. I hung the award on my cubicle wall years later when I sold real estate. Many of the agents never understood why.

Southern Wind

Long home from that journey
Here with Penelope happily at her loom
The color of last night still lovely in our cheeks
All is peace,
Yet in me there cries this restless voice
And though I somehow know better
Some part of me where my meanings are
Paces in the past, there only do I live.
To stand again on wooden, cold, high winded decks
Facing the North-West ice rains
Those sleeted tears from home
So alive, all that storied night
Pursuing the darkness,
Always full sail.
In sleep, I also dream of other times
And in that composed slice of death
I dream of thunder-red battle days,
Achilles at my side
Our strong, slashing, bloodied arms
Swinging fabled and great weighted swords,
Back to back, we denied the world
Access to our vulnerabilities.
Later, by the fire, on the reddened sands,
Tasting the wood-casqued home wine,

Mourning those whose lives have splintered,
I find I look with longing to the distant sea
And in my dream of war, I dream of home.

BILLY MCGEE AND THE COWBOYS

Billy McGee and I were kids together. Grade school, football, fights, bloody noses, scouts, and all that jazz. Billy was a better ballplayer, bigger and stronger, so the tears or bloody noses were all mine. Billy wasn't a bully in any way, but it never took much for me to rub him the wrong way, which was not a good thing to do as he was a pretty tough kid. But we were kids and lived on the same block. Sometimes we got along; sometimes, we did not, but to be honest, I have to admit his feelings for me as a kid were something he came by honestly.

After high school, I don't think we spent a lot of time together as he went right into the Air Force, and I went to work for a few years, college for a year, then into the army and off to Vietnam.

I had not seen Billy in almost 15 years when we ran into each other outside a funeral home in the town where we had grown up. Somebody we both knew had passed away. Neither of us lived in Ridley Park anymore. Billy, married with a small family, lived not far away. His wife, Marty, was pretty; they seemed happy. He was proud of his life, and I think he wanted me to see his home and all he had worked for, so I followed his car, and he led me to his house. It was a good time, one of the best I've had with him. I liked his wife and his home and was happy we'd run into each other again.

I was at the Vet at the time, the 70s, more or less in a holding pattern. Before I left, I offered to take Billy and his wife to a Phillies game sometime. Billy said he and Marty were not big baseball fans but, and then he paused and did that Billy McGee thing he always did when we were kids. He said I couldn't do it anyhow, so why bother to ask. I fell into the old trap of our "kid thing," and we went back and forth, with him not bringing up whatever it was and me saying: "Billy, what the hell is it?" We're standing in his driveway; this went on for quite a while. I found myself thinking, what the hell! Are we 11 years old again? Finally, it's really time to say goodbye and I tell him one more time, he and Marty should come up to the stadium for a game. Billy repeats one more time he knows I couldn't pull it off. We start round and round again like 11-year-olds until Marty calls him from the house for something and Billy finally blurts out, what he really would love, would be to go to an Eagles game, but not just any Eagles game. He and Marty would love to see the Eagles play the Dallas Cowboys. That, Billy said with certainly, was something I could not deliver. I took his number and told him I would call the week before the game and tell them where to meet me. Billy said that was a call he never expected to receive. Everything in the exchange echoed our childhood.

Eagles against Dallas was the hottest ticket in town, but I didn't need tickets. I had a key to the building and the connections to go with it. I called Billy the week before the game, asked him what car he'd be driving, and told him which gate to come to, that I'd find them. Billy, more than skeptical, did show up. I stood on the curb at the gate we referred to as "Pattison at The Vet" when Billy and Marty pulled up. I told the cashier, "He's cool," waved to the flagman, telling him to move the barricade, sending Billy and Marty into the VIP area reserved for Eagles team members, coaches, and staff parking. Billy, despite himself, was beaming. I put him in a spot between Jaworski's van and the fence.

Ron's van had a little cluster of nuts on the dash, a trio of little peanut-like figures singing, "Some days we're all a little nuts." That bit of high school whimsy was one of the many things I liked about Jaws.

I wasn't about to screw up my day with Marty and Billy by leaving anything to chance. I'd arranged things so I could get away from *the sturm und drang* of the lots for 10 minutes so I could take them inside as soon as they arrived. I escorted them through the door to the Stadium Club beneath Gate H. We hopped on the elevator to the club on the fourth floor. I took them past the line waiting to get in, introduced Billy to Carl, the maître d', and told him Billy was an old friend of mine. They were escorted to the table I'd reserved, one of the best tables in the house looking down from the fourth level above the Eagles' bench. When Joe DiMaggio was in the club for the 1980 World Series, his table was one tier above and behind Marty and Billy's table. They were on the glass. A lot of pregame activity was going on out on the field. Players from both sides were warming up. Punts were booming in the air. Quarterbacks were airing out "Hail Marys." I did not think I could have done more for them when I left them looking at the menu before they ordered brunch and drinks on my tab. Boy, was I wrong.

I didn't get back to them until just before the game started. My parking lots were under control, and the North lots were filled. I'd shifted the traffic patterns into the south lots. The pressure was off when I dropped in to see how my friends were doing. For October it was a bitterly cold day. I thought they'd be happy in their warm, comfortable seats with a great view of the game and the maître d' checking on them as if they were superstar celebrities. Carl's great at what he does.

Billy wasn't happy at all. He was anxious and wanted to know when they'd get to their seats. I told him these were their seats. They were sitting on the same level and 20 yards away from the super boxes of both Len Tose and The Mayor of Philadelphia, essentially sharing the same incredible view from the 400-level. I mean, how good can it get?

Something wasn't right. Neither Billy nor Marty were forthcoming. They didn't want to tell me, but they really longed to be out there in the crowd. They'd dreamed about being out in the weather with the fans, and it never occurred to me that maybe if once in your life you get to an Eagles game, an Eagles-Dallas game, you want the full experience, out in the stands, in the elements, comfort be damned. I wanted them to have a great experience. I'd blown it. I told them to sit tight. I would see what I could do. I was in scramble city.

I ran down to the 200-level seats in the section where all the players' wives sat and asked them if they could squeeze in two friends as a favor to me.

There were always a couple of empty seats in the wives' area, and the wives were only too happy to help me in a jam.

So, Billy and Marty finally attended a live Eagles Dallas game sitting in 200-level seats on the 40-yard line with the players' wives and girlfriends as the Eagles edged out the Cowboys in a 17-10 nail biter. I've hung out with these women in that section enough to know Billy and Marty were exposed to some incredible stories. I hadn't planned on them being in that section, but as it was their day, it couldn't have turned out better.

Or could it?

Once a year Albert Taxin, owner of the Olde Original Bookbinders at the foot of Walnut Street, hosted the team for a legendary after game feast. This was the night.

After the game, while their husbands were still getting wrapped in icebags and ace bandages, the wives were all heading to a townhouse on the corner of Fifth and Fitzwater Streets to change their clothes and get made up for the big night. Three of the Eagles, Giamonna, Spagnola, and Bunting lived there only two blocks from South Street. When I met Billy and Marty after the game, they thanked me profusely, excitedly telling me how well the wives treated them and how they'd never forget their totally bizarro world experience at the game. I had not thought of this before, but asked if they would like to go have a few beers with some of the wives and players at a pre-Bookbinder's party uptown. They didn't see this coming. I told them they could follow me up there. I had a key to 5th and Fitz. We were the first ones there, and they made themselves comfortable as I iced the beer and put out bowls of chips, pretzels, and dip. I had a key because the guys who lived there had a mattress on the floor of their heater room and let me sleep there whenever I got stir crazy from the solitude at the Vet. Sometimes I stayed there as much as at the stadium.

Wives arrived before their husbands and headed upstairs to do their hair and get all dolled up for the big night. Players started arriving in sport jackets with those big blue ice bags with white polka dots ace bandaged onto their knees or elbows. Marty was hanging out with a few of the girls she had gotten along with particularly well during the game. Not every player showed up, but there were probably at least a dozen couples there, and the house was abuzz with the close win over Dallas, the mood euphoric.

It was a great night, but it wasn't a late night, and Billy and Marty were among the last to leave. By 7:30, all the dinner guests had already headed up to the restaurant. But something happened earlier during the party that really made my day and put a cap on the yin and yang of my life experience with Billy McGee.

When most of the wives were upstairs getting all glammed up, I was standing at one end of the gigantic freestanding island in the kitchen, the house filled with music and laughter. At the far end of the island, I saw Billy standing between Keith Krepfle and John Spagnola, the Eagles' outstanding tight ends. They were good naturedly breaking each other balls about things one or the other had done during the game. It's one thing to see a game live or on television but it's another and profoundly deeper experience to stand between two key players not two hours after a contested game and listen to them discuss what they'd thought, felt, and done out on the field. Billy stood between them, and I could see they had accepted his presence as one of the crew. He was an affable and non-threatening fly on the wall, simply happy to be there. McGee had this look of rapture on his face I'd never seen before, and I loved it for him. Billy was as much a part of the good times at 5th and Fitz that night as anyone there. You could see it in his face. McGee was beaming. If I could have seen his aura it would have been a rich Eagles' Green with lightning flashes of white and silver. Billy looked like he was in the end zone of football heaven. He looked good there. He belonged in the moment. It was his; he owned it; he deserved it. I was happy for him.

I yelled, "Yo, Billy." He looked up, saw me, and smiled. The living description of a "grin from ear to ear." "So, I can't get you into an Eagles-Dallas game?" He laughed, raising his beer bottle in salute. Spag and Krepps weren't paying attention, lost in their moments of "instant replay" but Billy's raised bottle caught their attention as well as their euphoric mood. Grinning, they raised their bottles in a three-way clink with Billy. I can almost hear the sound of their bottles as I think of them.

Maybe McGee and I were 11 years old again, but the expression on Billy's face told me all was right with the world.

THE FOG

The only sport not covered up til now in these stories from my time at the Vet is hockey, and the tenuous threads that come together to form this bizarre anecdote are as off the wall as anything I've thrown at you. In 1967, my brother David and his wife Karen lived in an apartment after they got married. Their building was directly behind The Frosty Mug, a fast-food birch beer and burger drive-in on Chester Pike in Ridley Park. David called our brother Jimmy telling him he suspected some hockey players on the new hockey team in Philly might be living in their building. Dave noticed some cars in the lot with Canadian license plates and some stickers on their windows indicating the owners might be involved in hockey. David's suspicions were correct, and it turned out Joe Watson and Doug Favell were roommates sharing a ground-floor apartment in David and Karen's building. Favell and Watson were two members of the original Flyer's team with the solid hockey chops to contribute to our 1974 and 1975 Championships though Doug Favell was no longer a member of either Championship team. Before the 1974 season began, Favell was traded to the Maple Leafs for...wait for it...Bernie Parent.

Philadelphia didn't have a large following when the Flyers first came to town in 1967, so when Joe Watson opened his door and found two local kids who were fanatical about the game standing there with one of our mother's legendary hot milk sponge cakes, they invited the kids in, and a friendship began that exists to this day.

For every home game in the 1967 and 1968 seasons, Doug and Joe left two tickets for Kevin and Jimmy. My brothers never missed a game, and the seats were excellent. Jimmy and Kevin sat with the wives and Flyer's executives in some of the best seats in the house.

Jimmy and Kevin lived in our family home on Ridley Lake. They loved hockey and came from a line that produced one of the area's best amateur players, their Uncle Bob Nilon. Bob not only won the prestigious Hobey Baker Award back in the late 1930s playing for Saint Nick's in New York, but was slated to be on the American hockey team in the 1940 Olympics had Hitler not scrambled the world's eggs. Bob had been Most Valuable Player on an American Hockey Team that toured Europe in the early 1930s and won a major tournament in Bavaria. After their victory, Bob and his teammates were half-undressed when he was told to get out on the ice to receive the MVP Honor. All those kids wanted to do was get out on the town, chase frauleins and drink German beer. Bob, grumbling as he saw his teammates run off into the night, put his uniform back on and did as he was told, skating out to center ice where local officials hung the medal around his neck beneath large banners adorned with swastikas. They posed for photos, giving Bob the Nazi salute. Bob threw the medal in his hockey bag, forgot about it, and ran out to find his friends.

Ten Years later he was called before a Board of Inquiry while serving in the South Pacific to explain an enlarged photo of his MVP presentation found adorning the wall of a sports' bar in Munich. The German politician who draped the medal around his neck and gave Bob the Nazi salute was Adolph Hitler. I know for a fact that some version of this story ended up in a Delaware County newspaper, The Chester Times.

Now Bob's story is a major digression from my Vet Stadium

stories, but fleshes out my family's hockey background and shows why Kevin and Jimmy were more than predisposed to become serious hockey players. Because of Bob, my brothers learned the importance of stick handling and solid skating skills. Well before the time the Flyers brought big time ice hockey to Philadelphia and captured the hearts and imagination of Philly sports fans, my youngest brothers, who lived on Ridley Lake, had been out on the ice every time it was strong enough to hold them. If Kevin and Jimmy weren't in school or sleeping, they were chalking up "ice time" and fine-tuning their skills with countless drills Bob taught them.

Jimmy went off to play varsity hockey, football, and lacrosse for four years at Norwich University in Vermont and Kevin ended up playing hockey for St. James High School in a newly formed Inter-County High School League where Kevin stood out as the highest-scoring player in the entire league on a team that never won a single game. Mull that one over. Kevin also played for Widener University as a ringer on a club team although he wasn't a student there.

In 1975, after Fred Shero coached the Flyers to their second consecutive Stanley Cup victory, Fred began a summer hockey camp for kids. Gary Dornhoefer and Billy Clement were full-time partners, but many Flyers made short visits or cameo appearances. Jimmy Garvey heard about the camp and volunteered to work for nothing because he knew he'd learn a great deal and hone his coaching skills. Jimmy, teaching phys-ed and coaching Ridley High's Hockey Team, impressed Shero with his energy and love of the game and got the job. Within a few weeks, the only issue Coach Shero had with Jimmy was that he wasn't being paid, so Shero began paying Jim out of his own pocket. At the end of the summer Jimmy was called into a meeting with a very somber Shero, Dorney and Clement because there was a problem. They had just fired the director of the camp. Jimmy did not understand at first and asked if they were unhappy with his work. He was told they were not unhappy with his work at all. They were incredibly happy with his contribution, and that was the problem. The problem was he wasn't on salary, and they asked him to return the following year, but as director of the camp. Jimmy had gone from a walk-on volunteer to the director of the camp in ten weeks.

Jimmy worked for Fred Shero for all four years the hockey camp remained in business, the first year as a volunteer and then director of the camp for the next three years.

1978 was the final year for the hockey camp as Fred Shero left Philadelphia to be head coach of the New York Rangers. Jimmy and Fred Shero remained close friends until Fred died in 1990.

Here are two stories Jimmy shared with me about Fred Shero that will offer insight into the enigmatic man often referred to as "The Fog."

Fred Shero, The Flyers third coach in their first six years, only played two years in the NHL with the NY Rangers. Most of his experience was as a player and coach in the minors out West, but people who knew hockey understood Shero was a winner. In 13 years coaching in the minors, Fred compiled an impressive record of five "firsts," six "seconds" and two "thirds" in various leagues.

In 1971 Fred Shero became the head coach of the Philadelphia Flyers, and one of the first things he did was reinstall a soda machine in the locker room. This may not seem like a big deal, but it was. The previous coach, Vic Stasiak, was a hard-ass Ukrainian who thought soda machines in the locker room made players soft and were too permissive. His coaching style was right out of the 1930s and he treated his players like they were kids. Stasiak's style of coaching hadn't worked very well, and he only lasted two years. Shero not only brought back the soda machine but stocked it with beer as well.

Ed Snider got wind of this and stormed into the locker room, demanding the soda machine be removed immediately. When he discovered there was beer in the soda machine as well, he became apoplectic. Shero stood his ground, telling the red-faced team owner, "I'm the coach. You hired me to win games. If I don't produce a winner, you can fire me." Snider backed down, and Shero coached the Flyers to back-to-back Stanley Cups for Philadelphia.

In 1975, after Jimmy worked for Shero at his hockey camp, Kevin and Jimmy, wearing suits and ties, sat on the steps outside of the Ovations entrance to the Spectrum where players and coaches entered the building before games. They waited for Freddy to arrive for the game that evening. They'd been there since before 3 o'clock. Fred shows up, says hello and after a few pleasantries the boys ask Fred if they can walk in with him, riding on his coattails. Fred says, "Sure, follow me" and they walk in behind him. Shero goes through security but the guard on duty, who had also been a Philadelphia Policeman and Rizzo's personal bodyguard, steps in front of them holding up a large hand saying, "You can't come in without a ticket or a pass. No exceptions!" Fred stops, turns around and says to the guard, "They are with me! I am their ticket."

Once inside, Fred says, "It's really early, so you better stay in the locker room and my office at this time because if you are out in the arena without a ticket, you will be asked to leave the building. Stay here, and I'll bring you a couple of beers." It was as good a way to sneak into the Flyers game as possible. Hiding out in Shero's Office and drinking beer. From time to time, Jimmy and Kevin "snuck" into Flyers' games riding on Fred Shero's coattails.

Fred was their ticket.

THE CHICKEN RUN

One other thing I inherited from my cousin Terry was the chicken run. When the New York Rangers hockey team came to play the Philadelphia Flyers, the Rangers always referred to their road trip as "Heading down to 'Chicken Town.'" It was not a disparaging name for Philadelphia but a reference to something that happened every time they played at the Spectrum.

The Rangers always came South as a team on a chartered bus, and after the game, the bus was stocked with beer and sodas and buckets of fried chicken for the ride back to the Big Apple. It was a deal between two old friends, Bob Nilon and Emile Francis of the New York Rangers. The chicken run started long before I came on the scene. The chicken run had been Terry's responsibility, and when I replaced him, it came with the job. The chicken run was a royal pain in the ass.

The "Run" always made a long day longer. Instead of being done with work an hour or so after the hockey game began, it meant hanging around for a few hours before heading down to Gino's below the airport for a load of chicken. Timing was everything; the chicken had to be hot. Ice cold beer was easy but cold fried chicken was out of the question and if you cut it too close on the back end trying to deliver the hottest chicken possible, you could be late. The bus wouldn't wait. A nightmare scenario would be to roll into the

Spectrum parking lot with twenty buckets of fried chicken only to find the spot at the top of the ramp vacant where the bus had been.

AN OLD PAIR OF COWBOY BOOTS

I have an old pair of cowboy boots. Had them over 40 years. I don't wear them often but when I do somebody often makes a comment about them. Got a great deal on them too. I think they were listed around $300 when I got them back in the late 70s. I paid a little more than $100. Deal was, several times a year, Otho Davis, head trainer for the Philadelphia Eagles, would leave his battered copy of a Nocona Boots catalog around the locker room. Word got out Otho was putting an order together. Guys would grab the catalog, pick out some boots, add their names to a list, and give Otho the cash. Everybody with access to Otho's catalog always had great boots.

My boots are Nocona Anaconda Python snakeskin boots. I doubt that I'd order that kind of boot today, but that was a long time ago, and things were different. The boots still look pretty good. There's a tiny hole on the side of the left boot, half the size of a dime. I took them to DiMartino's Shoe Repair in Chestnut Hill that has been there since Woodrow Wilson was President. Generations of the same family passing their skills down to their children. Jimmy DiMartino loved the boots but said there was little he could do. So I've learned to live with the minor flaw. Sometimes an imperfection can be overlooked if you don't have any other choice. I love my old boots.

So, I'm out in a bar. I'm wearing my boots. Somebody notices them, makes a comment, and we get to talking boots, life, and all kinds of things. Often it comes around to "Where'd you get your boots?" I say, South Philly. If they ask where, I just tell them my boot paradise got blown up and turned into a parking lot, sounding a lot like a line from a song.

BILL SOUP

Can't take you into the Vet as I knew it without a piece on the greatest ballplayer, I knew from my time there. Bill Bradley had been given the nickname "Super Bill" by his teammates in High School. In an interview with Sport's Illustrated, he was asked if the kids really called him Super Bill. Typical Billy, he blew it off saying, "Most of the time, they just call me 'Soup'." To this day, some of his closest friends still call him: "Soup."

Bill Soup wasn't the biggest, strongest, or fastest guy on The Eagles, but on any football, basketball, or baseball team he ever played on in his prime, Billy was the best total package and a sheer joy to see in action. Sisemore told me when Billy was in high school, "They used to come from miles around and hang from the rafters to see Bill Soup play basketball."

And basketball was not his best sport.

Billy's best sport was probably baseball. He regretted, as he grew older, that he hadn't pursued a career on "the diamond," but it wasn't in the cards. He would have been a Hall of Famer. Billy had been smacking a ball around his backyard since he was two years old. You could see his potential that long ago, and as he grew up, everyone in his hometown knew he had the chops to make it to the big show. Any big show! They were not wrong.

In his excellent "Eagles Encyclopedia," Ray Didinger said, "As a free safety, Bradley had two major assets: (1) great instincts that were developed as a do-it-all quarterback at Palestine High School and (2) sure hands. He used his instincts to get to the football and his pickpocket hands did the rest." The best description of Bradley, according to Didinger, was offered by Hall of Fame quarterback Sonny Jurgensen, who described Bradley as being "Like a ghost. He's there, but you don't see him until it is too late." Didinger quoted Bradley saying, "One play sticks out in my mind, we were playing the Cardinals, and a receiver named John Gilliam came across the middle. I saw the ball in the air and broke on it. We came together, Gilliam and me, and I just took the ball away. On the films you can see one guy really wanted the ball and the other guy didn't. That's how I remember my career. I was the guy who wanted the ball."

Soup's father, Joe Sephus Bradley, wanted Bill to have a better life than he'd known and insisted Bill get a college education. This insistence and respect for his father's wishes combined to lead him to accept a full scholarship to The University of Texas in Austin. Texas is football country, and every kid's dream in Bill's era would be to go to Austin and be coached by the legendary Darrell Royal. A full ride to UT was high cotton! As a senior, Billy led The Palestine High School "Wildcats" football team to win the state championship. If you asked any guy on any of his teams back then what he was like, they'd tell you from deep in their hearts that he was just one of them. He never thought of himself as better than anyone, but there was no one like him. Bill had played every minute of every game that got them there.

But Bradley's Wildcats almost didn't make it to the State Championship.

On December 12th, 1964, Palestine High School in East Texas was closing in on its first-ever shot at The State Championship. To this day, it remains Palestine's only successful run for the roses.

First, they had to get past a formidable undefeated team from Wichita Falls in the semi-finals. Bill Soup was considered to be the best all-around player in Texas. He ran and passed the ball, punted, returned kickoffs on offense and kicked off on defense and was the consensus best safety in the state. Darrell Royal showed up with a carload of coaches from UT to scout Billy B. Events like that, being what they are, leaked to the fans and everyone in the stadium knew about the VIPs in the press box.

The game was a disaster. Curtis Fitzgerald, Bill's "Go to" favorite receiver, had broken his right arm below the shoulder and had been fitted with an air cast and sent to the hospital. With less than eleven minutes left on the clock, the score was 23 to Zip and everyone knew Royal and his entourage had left for Austin before the 4th quarter, Palestine losing by more than three touchdowns, nothing to see here. Wichita Falls fans were celebrating. It was over.

But Fitzgerald had not gone to the hospital. Curtis Fitzgerald removed his cast and lied to his coach telling him the doctor had cleared him to play showing some of the ballsy grit he'd show a few years later as a highly decorated helicopter pilot in Vietnam, always completing his missions though often gravely wounded.

With almost ten minutes on the scoreboard clock, Bradley hit a quick slanting Fitzgerald and the wingback with a broken arm clawed his way to the Wichita 13-yard line, an electrifying 35-yard gain. The Wildcats scored on a Bradley pass and went for two. 23-8. Billy ran for the second touchdown, passing again for the two pointers: 23 to 16. The next touchdown, another pass, but the try for two was batted down. Palestine had always gone for two pointers all year, making 90% of them. The scoreboard showed Palestine down 23 to 22 with barely Four minutes on the clock. Billy Bradley had a scary feral look in his eyes.

The final drive by The Palestine Wildcats placed them in scoring position with two seconds on the clock. A maniacal Darrell

Royal stood in the back of the end zone, uncharacteristically hooting and waving his arms, rooting for The Wildcats. He'd been listening to the game on the radio. Royal's carload of coaches had driven like teenagers on a Saturday night, racing to get back to the game once they heard Billy engineering a miraculous comeback.

The end didn't come easy. Bill told Fitzgerald he had to come through one more time, but on the shortened field the Wichita Falls coverage was brutal. Billy ran right, nothing there. Soup switched passing hands and ran left, still nothing. The clock read 00:00. Switching his passing hand repeatedly, Billy ran right, then left again, side arming a "Hail Mary" left hander to Curtis in a scrum of Wichita jerseys. No time on the clock. Soup paid dearly for his effort in late dirty hits. His helmet so twisted on his head one eye was looking through the ear hole. He didn't know how it turned out until the refs untangled the cursing scrum in the end zone. Fitzgerald had the ball. He held it up like the trophy it was and flashed a well-earned "cat that got the canary" grin.

Darrell Royal has always insisted, "It was the greatest effort I've ever seen in my life, high school, college or pro." Bill Soup and his Wildcats were going to the State Championship.

Bill Bradley's Palestine Wildcats defeated San Marcos to win the Texas High School State Championship 24 to 15 with Super Bill Bradley demonstrating once again that he not only deserved his nickname but clearly was the best all-around high school football player in Texas. Soup played all sixty minutes and contributed two touchdown passes, a rushing TD, three two pointers and three interceptions as a freezing blue norther ripped through Texas A & M's Kyle Field.

Darrell Royal said, "Bill Bradley might just be the best player to ever suit up for The Longhorns." He still holds two University of Texas school records from the 1960s: most interceptions in one game, four, and longest punt, 72 yards. Soup held a "most yards total offense" record until Earl Campbell took that honor in 1977. It's fitting that Royal once said the best two athletes he ever coached in his career were Bill Bradley and Earl Campbell, "The Tyler Rose."

Coach Royal did not allow Bill to play any other sport at UT but in an interview when Soup was at UT, the head basketball coach, asked to name the best basketball player on his team, said "Undoubtedly the best basketball player on campus is Bill Bradley." Soup wasn't even on the team.

And as I said, "Basketball wasn't even Billy's best sport."

I never saw Billy play ball. For whatever reason, I was in an alternate universe in the earliest years after Vietnam and did not follow any sports till I was dragged into the Vet by fate, desperation, and family ties. When I began to meet players in the N1 section of the north lot where they parked for games or practice, I started paying attention to what they were doing, not because they were professional athletes and I was a fan, but more as likable guys I met at work who became friends. A handful of them helped me along the way when I was more at risk from a meltdown than anyone realized. Bradley, Sizemore, Osborne, Tautolo, Papale, Bunting, Spagnola, and Giamonna were there for me when I needed shelter, friends, or kindness. It turned out I had taken Vince Papale's hotty sister, Janice, to my senior prom at Saint James, in 1961, almost 20 years earlier. Some of the guys understood me more than others, but all accepted me in ways I needed at the time to stay reasonably sane. The 1970s and the first few years in the '80s were incredibly difficult for me, and in ways most of those guys never fully understood they helped me to stay mentally afloat. My own worst enemy, I wasn't a victim of anything. We all need someone to lean on. Nobody really makes it all on their own. "No man is an island."

These men and their families did more for me and meant more

to me than they will ever understand.

I met Bill Soup for the first time at the Vet after his playing days. Ozzie introduced us. We hung out, grew close, and are best friends. There's something humble and spectacular about this guy. It's an ineffable thing. If you know Billy, you will get this and understand how all words fall short.

Billy's "Super" for certain, but he possesses an uncanny and deep human insight into team dynamics. There is a photograph of Palestine's High School Team taken the night they won the state championship. He played 60 black and blue minutes and Billy's hands touched the ball for every point scored. "Best in Texas" is high cotton indeed. Billy stepped out of the limelight and credited his buddies with a team effort win. In the photo at the very back of the room are Curtis Fitzgerald and Bill Bradley. Anyone who ever played with Billy has always said the same thing; he was just one of us who never thought of himself as being special in any way. The fans always loved Billy, and Billy loved them back.

One time we came across the Walt Whitman Bridge. I was driving, Billy in the passenger seat. As I stopped to pay the toll, the guy in the booth yelled "Bill Bradley" and jumped out and ran around the front of my pickup. Billy jumped out too, and they began dancing around and laughing like kids running under an open fire hydrant on a summer day. Billy knew the guy's name and all about his family. It was old home week until the blast of horns from behind crashed their party. Billy knew everybody and had time and interest for everyone he met.

And Billy loved The Vet.

I remember one time we walked into the stadium together, nothing going on, maybe baseball that night, but I cannot remember. We lingered awhile talking to "Mister C" at the door near the elevator over by gate H. Loveable Mister Cassidy, an elderly security guard, a charming guy with a smile that could light up a scoreboard. We never blew through that door without spending a few minutes catching up.

We went inside, crossing the inner concourse to the top of the 200-level seats, leaning on the rail looking down on the field. The Stadium was set up for baseball, but I don't think there was a game that night, nobody around, everything quiet. A building that roars during games now hushed in repose, absolutely and totally quiet. Not eerie, but somehow sacred by all that's ever happened there. Streaks of late afternoon sun stretched across the outfield. I loved the Vet like this. Billy did too. We stood there a long time, silently staring up into the upper level, lost in our thoughts.

I finally asked, "Billy, can you hear them?"

Staring hypnotically up into the 700 level, Billy didn't turn to me when he spoke.

"Yeah. Yeah... I do. I'll always hear them."

Bill Soup was there for me at the end of my time at the Stadium. In 1981 a new contract was offered under competitive bidding and Nilon Brothers, knowing all the operational costs and expenses, made a reasonable bid close to their 14.9 cents on the dollar based on a two-dollar parking fee but lost the contract to a new bidder. It wasn't even close. The new bidder won the contract with a low bid of under 12 cents on the dollar. Within months of the new contractor taking over, The City of Philadelphia increased the parking fee to three dollars for all events at the sports complex. Somebody knew something Nilons didn't.

It did not matter, my time at the Vet was over.

My last event at the Vet was a wildcard playoff loss to the Giants on the 27th of December 1981.

I closed the apartment and turned in my keys to the kingdom.

In mid-February, 1982, Billy Bradley showed up in Philadelphia with his late father's brown 1952 Chevy pickup truck to take some furniture Bill had in storage back to Texas. Billy called me. We ended up at Walt's Crabs on Two Street with a buddy, Mike Studzinski. "Studo" had been working construction nearby.

Billy asked me what I was doing. I didn't have any plans or prospects. Billy asked me to come back to Texas and hang out for as long as I liked. He had a place in Austin where he was living with Margaret Brown. I knew this "Tyler Rose," liked her and got along well with her. They had an extra bedroom. I came up with a lot of lame reasons why I couldn't get away, but they didn't pass the smell test. Billy said he would be outside my parent's house at 7: 30 the following morning. When he beeped the horn, I'd better come out, or he was going to drag me out.

"So, you're telling me you're going to kidnap me and take me to Texas, whether I want to go or not?"

Billy smiled and drank his beer. "You will have the time of your life." On the 16th of February 1982, the old Brown pickup truck pulled up in front of my family home on Ridley Lake. I got in. The day damp, miserable, and gray, temperature hovering in the teens.

Seven days later, on a Sunday afternoon, Billy and I rolled into Austin. The skies were blue; the temperature pushing 96°. People were swimming in Zilker Park. The trip with two drivers could have been covered easily in two days, three max, but Soup doesn't always travel in straight lines. I didn't come home from Texas until the night before Christmas.

Billy was right. I had the time of my life.

To anyone who ever enjoyed Bill Bradley as a ball player on any team, at any time, I enthusiastically and strongly urge them to read Jim Dent's excellent book *The Kids Got It Right* which details Bill's high school career and "The Big 33" game in Hershey, Pennsylvania. It's an incredible story, well told.

THE STADIUM CAT

…was a nickname given to me by John Turner, a friend of Pat Nilon's one night during the seventh inning stretch. A cat ran out on the field while everybody was standing up and singing, "Take me out to the ball game." The cat seemed to come out from somewhere between the end of the visiting team's dugout and the spot where the ball girl sat by the picnic area fence down the left-field line.

The cat realized it wasn't anywhere it wanted to be once it wandered out on the field a little bit past a point of comfortable return and couldn't get back to whatever hole it came from. "Froggy" and his groundskeeper's crew were on the field during "the stretch," grooming the dirt areas around the bases, and some of them were chasing the cat. They were no match for a frightened cat with an entire major league ball field to run loose in. It was a show. The fans were loving it. Richie Ashburn said something about, "The stadium cat is on the loose…." And Turner turned to me, saying, "That's a good name for you, the stadium cat." In some circles the name stuck, and friends laughingly referred to me by that name.

So, here's to our Vet and all the great memories so many of us had from our time there. There are markers in the parking lot not far from the Northeast corner of Broad and Pattison indicating where home plate, the bases, and pitcher's mound were in the old stadium. I once walked and roughly measured the 300-foot distance from home plate to the approximate location of the left-field foul ball pole. I then added another 40 feet for good measure to stand as close as possible on the spot where once, for a brief and unforgotten time, friends and I hung out in a place known to us as the Secret Apartment.

I stood on the spot I estimated to be closest to my old secret apartment with a cold beer. I poured a libation to Zeus on the blacktop before savoring a drink, thinking of old friends, many gone now, and some great memories which will belong to many of us down all our days. I tell you this with no shame or embarrassment: I stood there laughing until I cried.

Reflecting on that time from the advantage of a saner life, I must admit I perversely enjoyed the "Phantom of The Opera" aspect of my life in the Vet. All in all, I loved it. Oh God, I loved it and a lot of Eagles and Phillies fans out there reading this would've loved it too.

If I were the same person I was at that time in my life, I probably would do it all over again. It was a solitary time in so many ways but gave me time for sobering introspection and I came out of it changed for the better in ways I had never foreseen.

I thought I lived in the Vet because I could, but it became something more for me. I came to understand that in the end I lived in the Vet not because I could but because I had to. I needed a place of healing and my nights alone with her helped bring about the peace of mind needed to move on to the next and best stage of my life. Roller skating the 600-level, hypnotically losing myself in rotating views of the city or sitting for long periods in the dark at the top of the 700-level prepared me for the next chapters in my life. I somehow knew that one day in my not too distant future I would meet a woman who would need and love me as much as I would need and love her.

Once on the Cambodian Border, I had calmed my little band of Montagnards when we were surrounded and outnumbered about ten to one in an enemy base camp. I told them that there would be "Many Beaucoup Magics" that day and somehow, we would survive, and everything would be okay. Like Thoreau leaving Walden Pond, I left the stadium because I had other lives to live, and it was time to go and live them. I had a book I felt obligated to write and a great love to find and share my life with, and all this came to pass.

Years later when I watched the Vet implode, I thought of the cats, some of whom must still be in the stadium, and I felt sad for them as I felt a profound and deep sense of loss for the Vet so many of us loved which would be no more.

I was the Stadium Cat that got away....

ABOUT THE AUTHOR

Tom Garvey, an Airborne, Ranger, and Special Forces Officer served as an A- team leader in Vietnam in 1968 and returned home in late January 1969 to mixed reviews about his stability and state of mind. Like many other Vietnam Veterans, Tom found few who cared to hear about his time overseas. Within one week of his homecoming, he was a full-time college student during the day while working midnight to 8 AM, six days a week in the Blade Shop at Westinghouse Electric in Lester, Pennsylvania. In 1971 he graduated magna cum laude from Widener University in Chester, Pennsylvania. After college, the kindest way to put it is that "the wheels came off" and he managed to survive with menial jobs until he met the love of his life, Peggy Bertholf. One of his jobs was as a cashier/supervisor in the parking lots surrounding Vet Stadium. Eventually, reluctantly, and by default, Tom became the parking operations manager of all events at the Philadelphia Sports Complex and lived in a "Secret Apartment" in Veterans Stadium for several years. In 1982 Tom was "kidnapped" by Super Bill Bradley and taken to Texas for 11 months before returning to Philadelphia. From the day Tom met Peg, in 1983, he sensed he had finally come home. He married for the first time at the age of 50 and is blessed with a wonderful family of five stepchildren and their mates and two world-class granddaughters. Tom credits Peg's influence, love, and never faltering belief and support as the sole reason he was able to complete his lifetime dream of writing the critically acclaimed Many Beaucoup Magics.

Life is good. Life is incredibly good, indeed. Tom has finally come home.

"And in my dream of war, I dream of home."
"Southern Wind"

CRITICAL REVIEWS OF
MANY BEAUCOUP MAGICS

"An ambitious debut novella that offers a Vietnam war story with a clever plot device involving astrology, dreams, and omens. The climax is a scene which begs for the big screen treatment. Overall, Garvey writes tightly and economically with hardly a wasted word, when so many other Vietnam books tend to sprawl. A slightly different kind of Vietnam tale by a gifted writer.

~ The Kirkus Review, Many Beaucoup Magics, 2015

"A beautiful and touching combination of the physical, mental and philosophical war for a man's soul."

~ Hugh Gilmore, author of "My Three Suicides, A Success Story."

"I received this book from a friend two days ago and barely put it down until the end. It's a slim volume, but a very big story. Garvey takes us on a mystical journey as old as time, a young man's discovery of war and what it really means. Garvey's terse style and relentless pacing help us smell the jungle, feel the heat, and join with McManus and the Montagnard tribes he leads towards an unavoidable fate. If there has been a better study of a young soldier coming to terms with himself since Crane's The Red Badge of Courage, I haven't read it. Many Beaucoup Magics indeed."

~ Jeff Wilson, Amazon Review, July 2018

Made in the USA
Middletown, DE
12 June 2021